*Taking Power*

## OTHER TITLES FROM NEW FALCON PUBLICATIONS

# Taking Power

**Claiming Our Divinity Through Magick**

by
Stephen Mace

NEW FALCON PUBLICATIONS
TEMPE, ARIZONA, U.S.A.

International Standard Book Number: 1-56184-240-0
Library of Congress Catalog Card Number: 2005929465


First Edition 2005

To contact the Author write to:
Stephen Mace
P.O. Box 256
Milford, CT 06460-0256
U.S.A.

Those expecting a reply should enclose a stamped, self-addressed envelope. Foreign correspondents should enclose international reply coupons.

The paper used in this publication meets the minimum requirements of the American National Standard for Permanence of Paper for Printed Library Materials Z39.48-1984

Address all inquiries to:
NEW FALCON PUBLICATIONS
1739 East Broadway Road #1-277
Tempe, AZ 85282 U.S.A.

(or)
320 East Charleston Blvd. #204-286
Las Vegas, NV 89104 U.S.A.

website: http://www.newfalcon.com
email: info@newfalcon.com

**For Jerry, Chuck & Bert**

# Table of Contents

# Introduction

In October of 1970 I underwent an irrevocable magickal initiation. This was not done under the aegis of any high priest or magus, no possessor of the Secret Keys, but at the entirely oblivious hands of the Civil State, wielding all its panoply of guns, chains and iron cages. Though practically devoid of esoteric symbolism, this initiation followed all the forms: the threat of death, the ritual binding, the period of death/gestation in the tomb/womb and, upon release, the instruction by the Hierophant. Since this initiation was entirely unintentional, its consequences have been entirely unavoidable. That is, if I had *decided* to undergo a formal initiation, I could later *decide* that my initial reasoning had been misinformed and reject or "place in perspective" the whole experience, effectively escaping it. But with the State doing it, such rationalizations are unavailable. The Lord Initiating was no man of flesh and blood whom I could refute or lose faith in. My choices never had anything intellectual about them, and escape was not an option. There was only the stark alternative of courage or cowardice. Cowardice did not seem consistent with long-term survival.

Thus from the beginning my approach to power has been dynamic rather than symbolic, simply because I had to deal with the dynamics before I knew anything about the symbols. The Tarot deck that predicted the police raid—thus giving it its unmistakable magickal subtext—was that of Arthur Edward Waite, but I only knew the Nine of Swords was bad because the card reader said so. And when he gave me my instruction after my release, his description of Qabalah was unconvincing, but his copy of Aleister Crowley's *Eight Lectures on Yoga* was fascinating. There was no need

9

for Qabalah there, nor in any other part of magick, once a later teacher introduced me to the work of Austin Osman Spare. For me it was the way power worked that had to be understood. The symbols are just tools to manage it once we have it to dispose of.

This is the attitude that informs the contents of this book, which—with the exception of "On the Virtuous Wizard"—first appeared in book form as Part One of *Addressing Power*. Every chapter but the one on omens was first published in a journal of magick—English, German or American—and always it has been my intent to make the dynamics of magick perfectly clear, along with the techniques for manipulating them, so anyone able to will, dare and keep silent could apply them. Regardless of our symbolic orientations, power behaves the same way for us all. If we can learn the details of working it, whichever symbols we use to apply it can be so effective as to imply they are the Exclusive Truth of the Creator of the Universe.

But since each of us help create the world each instant, in the end this wouldn't be such a huge exaggeration at all.

I must thank a number of people for their help and encouragement in my pursuit of this enterprise. These include Ray Johnson, Glenn Behrle, the von Hofe family and Richard Corey for their material and intellectual support, and AShN55; Katon Shual 93; Atrox .808.; Daniel Alvin; Ray Sherwin, P.D. Brown, Dave Lee, Phil Hine and Ian Read; and Frank Cebulla[1] for giving me a reason to do the work. Our profits may have been minimal, but there was a certain glory in it, and a chance at an enduring influence. That chance is still good.

---

[1] Editors of the journals *Vitriol, Nuit-Isis, Thanateros, Widdershins, Chaos International*, and *Der Golem.*

# Spirits and Their Training

Magick is a psychic technology, a way to manipulate psychic energy so it will behave in accordance with our wills.

There are two ways to experience psychic energy—either we can be possessed by it or else we can regard it objectively, and hence have the option of control. When we are possessed by psychic energy, it does what psychic energy does: it energizes the action of our psyches. It can inspire intellectually, spiritually, or artistically; it can empower metabolically or sexually; it can overwhelm emotionally—all depending on the type of energy it is and the way we process it. On the other hand, when we deal with it objectively, we can treat it as a separate "stuff" that moves through and may be manipulated within space, that can be set onto a target and then cut off so it sticks to it. Once we have mastered the necessary technique, we can conjure psychic energy, accumulate it, store it, transport it, banish it, shield it, or dissipate it. We can discern its presence and read its nature through its effects on events and human activity. We can develop our psychic anatomies to make ourselves fit tools to manipulate it in any way we desire.

Though psychic energy surely finds its most efficient application when the magician uses it to manipulate his or her own self, its action is more startling when it discharges as an objective event. When the power is built up purposefully in the hope that such a discharge will occur, this is conjuring, and it is successful to the extent that an event occurs that promotes one's purpose. When the discharge is accidental, perhaps because of a build-up of which the principals were entirely unaware, then the event is an omen. In such a case the apparently random display will, through its precise timing, display its connection with its subject matter, and through its own analogous content will make a precise comment upon the nature of the power build-up within this subject, and its likely avenue of discharge.

Divination with cards, coins, shells or runes is simply the use of a random symbol generator that is sensitive enough to produce omens from the slightest psychic stress.

Magick is thus the general term for the deliberate manipulation of psychic energy. But if we are to get a real grip on it, we have to be more specific. Traditionally the way to control psychic energy has been to treat it sorcerously. Sorcery works on the assumption that each definably distinct aspect of psychic energy is a separate, self-aware "spirit," an individual entity with whom the sorcerer enters into a personal relationship. The sorcerer regards the spirit as if it were an individual "person" that acts to perform a specific psychic task. By definition (or convention), any mental function you can specify—be it conscious, unconscious or a combination of the two—may be regarded as a separate spirit, a personality with a name whom you may bind to your will. Sorcerous thinking holds that the human personality is a cluster of spirits more or less under the control of a central column of awareness and will. In essence the relationship is a feudal one; you are the lord and your spirits are your vassals, and through them you assert your mastery over your domain. Sorcery thus provides the option of re-engineering psyche through the manipulation of these spirits, whose dynamics collectively determine personality and behavior. And as the sorcerer gains power, he or she will learn to recognize psychic energy *as such*, and so manipulate it in those terms. As Austin Spare put it, he or she will liberate desire from belief, and then ride it like a shark through an ocean of self-love.

On the other hand, we all know it's possible to get by without sorcery, taking our spiritual apparatuses as circumstances determine without any interest in manipulating their internal structures or using them to manage spiritual energies in the outside world. We can even find systems of belief—Christianity, for example—which can help the faithful manipulate psychic energy without requiring them to deal with their internal psychic structures at all. But such devotional techniques restrict our options by the types of devotion they demand and by their quite limited techniques for dealing with the energy once it is obtained. For sheer freedom of movement, there is no substitute for defining each aspect of power separately, binding it so it will obey one's word, and then enhancing it or diminishing it as one's will might determine.

But then this much is obvious, and should win agreement from sorcerers of all schools. Where sorcerers in general more or less disagree is on the architecture of personality, how the spirits that make it up are best sorted out and labeled, and how they may be best bound and manipulated. The result is a welter of systems, all evolving and influencing one another over time, from the earliest ages to the present. Certainly many of these symbolic conventions for spiritual labeling have in the process reached heights of maturity and elegance, but they are still all projections from the past that we impose upon our brand-new present. They are also all more or less dogmatic, and so more or less restrictive, and of the essence of sin.

It would seem preferable simply to begin an open-minded exploration of one's spiritual landscape and deal with the powers one finds there as one finds them. This is the tack Austin Spare took, and to me it seems to be what makes Chaos magick what it is. For those who choose this unmapped path, the question then becomes: How can we tread it with courage and still live out our lives with our mental equipment reasonably intact?

I would answer: By taking care to center ourselves, by distinguishing our spirits well and truly, by binding them with full concentration and intent, and by using them in harmony with our individual True Wills—whatever it is that we must **do** to be who we truly are.

We need to be centered so we'll have a high ground to stand on, safe against attacks from both magickal enemies (rare) and our own demons (inevitable). The main work here is making banishing a daily habit, whether with a traditional rite like the pentagram ritual or some more abstract procedure, for instance one involving three interlocking rings of Light purged by an expanding column of fire. Advanced techniques include the identification and penetration of chakras, and circulation of the Light.

Sorting out our spirits is a less straightforward task. That it must be an individual effort is obvious. Everyone's karma, training and circumstances are different, so the composition of their spiritual sheaths will be also. And different wills must emphasize different aspects of personality. The spirits of a woman whose will it is to raise children will differ from those of a woman who would excel in crop dusting.

So we must do our psychic engineering on our own. To gain access to the levers and engines of psyche, sorcerers have recourse to a technique known as astral projection. The astral plane is a place where conscious purpose meets unconscious necessity. It is an interface of imagination between the conscious and the unconscious, a realm accessed through the separation in imagination of the astral body from the physical. Through the technique of astral projection, well-described in Aleister Crowley's *Magick in Theory and Practice*, we have a tool for meeting our spirits on their own ground. We may assert control there, but we must do so according to the rules of that ground, the natural laws that hold good there. For this reason Crowley lays great stress on proper procedure, including the need to banish before and after the working, the separation of bodies, the testing of spirits by imposing their proper symbols upon them, and the need for a thorough reunion of bodies. Because it is effective, astral projection can be dangerous if it is not done right. A neophyte should thoroughly study the technique before beginning, and this essay should be seen as only the briefest introduction to it.

Crowley began his own astral research with his symbolic map already drawn. From even before his initiation into the Golden Dawn, he was well-soaked in the Qabalistic theosophy, and his subsequent indoctrination by that Rosicrucian order branded the Tree of Life onto his deep psyche. Deep psyches are in general quite mutable within the bounds of their essential structures, and the Tree of Life is sufficiently adaptable that he was able to rely on it throughout his life. He even applied it to three systems that have little or nothing to do with Qabalah: Enochian, I Ching, and Thelema.

Crowley's defense of using a traditional system—in defiance of his usually strict scientific approach—is that the Tree of Life is merely a filing system, a descriptive convenience for sorting out spiritual phenomena and labeling them for discussion and use. He compared the elements of the Qabalistic system to the letters of the alphabet—insufficient to match perfectly all English sounds, but good enough for us to read the words. According to Crowley, the only possible objection to the Tree is that one could call it inconvenient. "One cannot call it incorrect."

By the same token, one could say that Ptolemy's earth-centered universe is not wrong, merely inconvenient, since his epicycles accurately predict the motion of the planets against the stars. And this analogy is relevant since the Tree of Life is not just a filing system, but also involves some intrinsic assumptions about the nature of power and our "proper" progress through it. Just as Ptolemy's universe is earth-centered, Qabalah carries with it a substantial Neoplatonic bias, and if you brand its symbolism onto your unconscious, you may brand it with that bias as well.

So is the Tree of Life then wrong? I don't choose to say so. For one thing, many people find it a system well-able to call up and handle power. For another, the individual approach to spiritual exploration is necessarily a lonely one, and group working can help to break one's solitude. But the only way we can work with or even talk to another magician is if we adopt a common language of convenience, a role in which the symbols of the Tree function well.

Of course systems like the Tree also help by providing frameworks we can rely upon as psychic support, predrawn maps that tell us where we're supposed to go and the traps we're likely to meet on the way. That a wizard is thus bound to the map and its progress upwards is the price he or she pays for its stability and good sense. For those of us who don't choose to pay this price, the landscape is more darkly lit, but at least free of preconceptions. And if we must grope a bit more than our Qabalistic peers, we can still set our own pace, only calling our spirits to account when we feel confident we can dominate them. And which spirits may we call? Why, any we can define as callable!

An example here would serve us best.

Suppose a budding wizard has a hypercritical, self-righteous streak—a personality trait that any objective family member would say he inherited from his father. But suppose our neophyte—who was only six when the man died—has no understanding of this. To his mind the human race is incredibly slow and stupid, and needs some well-phrased correction if it's going to shape up. As he undergoes the disciplines of the magick path, he gains power. Eventually he acquires enough power that he gives the world such a sharp lesson that it takes notice of him and responds with a hard right to the back of his head. This causes him to undertake an astral projection for the purpose of confronting the spirit of his misfortune.

But the astral does not respond to mere wishes—rather to symbols and conjurations—and wizards need such if they are to use Crowley's method. Austin Spare recommended automatic drawing as a way to cause one's own deep psyche to design one's symbols (which he called "sacred letters"), and also suggested the use of an alphabetic sigil soaked with "free belief" to conjure with. Though Spare never wrote of astral projection, it is possible to adapt these methods to it, and they may be applied to any sort of spirit we may possibly imagine.

So how does our neophyte proceed? First he designs his sigil, perhaps from the phrase: "Why I am always getting fired." Leaving out the duplicates, this contains the letters:

WHYIAMLSGETNFRD

out of which he can make this sigil:

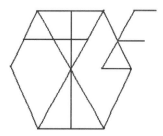

Thereafter, whenever he feels abused after being told to shut up and do his own work, he will simply turn away, collect his rage into a clear expression of the righteousness of his position, and then dismember it by applying the "Neither-Neither principle" to release the energy behind the rage in the form that Spare called "free belief." The Neither-Neither is based on the assumption that to assert any position as fact makes that position's opposite equally necessary. If one then opposes this opposite to the original, one will liberate the energy locked up in it. How much power their juxtaposition will release depends upon both the strength of the original passion and also how open-minded one is. Our neophyte could release a lot of power by forcing himself to recognize how his suggestions to his co-workers might be uninformed, irrelevant, wrong, or a plain nuisance. He could release just a little bit by telling himself that if the fools are too dense to admit his insight, he is obliged to leave them alone.

Either way, once free belief has been released it is available to charge the sigil, which our neophyte will do by using the power to make the sigil glow bright in his mind's eye. As the sigil begins to fade, he will seal this potential inside it by forcing the sigil out of his mind, purposefully repressing all thought of the monogram until he again has free belief available. Thus he causes the power to ferment in darkness, becoming organic and individual, ready to respond when he calls it to him.

As a tool for managing such a spirit, our neophyte will design what Spare called its "sacred letter," an ideograph which should represent the essentials of its nature. This figure may be superimposed on the astral form of the spirit to test it (impostors will shrivel and die) or compel its obedience. Sacred letters can be designed by means of automatic drawing: while he stares at his sigil the wizard's hand will doodle, sketch, or draw on its own, until it produces lines in which he recognizes the complex interaction of power that the spirit essentially is. He will confirm this shape with divinations and then prepare to meet it on the astral.

Depending on how open-minded our neophyte was as he went through his preparations, this meeting can come as more or less of a shock. If he began to suspect his father was part of it when he kept doodling a face like it was in the man's photographs, then he won't be surprised to see the man respond to the conjuration. On the other hand, if he expected to meet the cynicism that makes the world cruel, and instead finds his own asininity, with Dad's sarcastic wit egging it on, then he may be in trouble. If the shock is such that he is at all unsure of his power to dominate the demon, then he should banish immediately, reunite his bodies, and banish again. Then he should eat—this to close his chakras. Thus back safe in the mundane, he can meditate on his life in the light of this new insight, making a rational counter to the demon's attack on his emotions. He can also build up his aura with any centering exercises he might find useful. Then when he is confident of his position, he can go back onto the astral, call up the demon, and subject it to the Charge to the Spirit. The point is that he must be stronger than the spirit if he is to bind it, and he must be able to look it full in the face as he does so, seeing all the small crimes and tricks of fate that made it grow into what it is for him now. Only then will the Charge permeate it all, subjecting every aspect of the demon to his will.

Another ally that can be helpful in gaining the upper hand is the Holy Guardian Angel. The Holy Guardian Angel was first given its occult meaning by the alleged Abraham who wrote what S.L. MacGregor Mathers translated as *The Book of the Sacred Magic of Abramelin the Mage*. As Abraham has it, the Angel is the servant of the Lord God Almighty, who sends it to the wizard to serve as his or her personal advisor in all things spiritual—this after the wizard completes six months of prayer, devotion and study of the scriptures, followed by a week of conjurations. After the wizard has been instructed and empowered by his or her Angel, he or she will be able to command both the evil spirits and the good—this for the praise and glory of the Holy Name, for his or her own use, and for that of his or her neighbor.

Now as we all know, devotion to the Lord God Almighty and close structure of the scriptures are not now as popular as they were in the fifteenth century, even among mystic wizards, so there are now modern variations on Abramelin's technique. Some choose to employ purely ceremonial methods, for instance Crowley's all-consuming *Liber Samekh*. Others have used Spare's method of sigils, free belief, and sacred letters, even though Spare never mentioned the Holy Guardian Angel in his published work.

Personally, I first met my Angel through a combination of sigils and sacred letters similar to that just given. When I later adopted *Samekh* to cement our relationship, success came much more quickly due to my knowledge of my Angel's name, which I had gained from my initial efforts.

Once a wizard is conversant with his or her Angel, he or she will have access to the ultimate informant on things spiritual. The Holy Guardian Angel can provide the names and letters for the spirits needed for any operation, and back the wizard up when he or she binds them. His (or her) Angel will tell him when operations he'd like to do aren't in his best interest, and will do so in astral visions that are remarkably vivid and seem to have a life of their own. His Angel will spark his interest in lines of work he had not previously considered, but which are necessary for his progress. The wizard will find his Angel to be a fountain of Grace, Power and Good Advice, and he must be sure to treat it with utmost respect at all times. It is his direct link to the Highest—an ally, a benefactor, but never a servant.

In any event, once our neophyte can dominate his demon while standing to it face-to-face, then he is ready to Charge it, with or without the assistance of his Angel. For this he must simply meet it on the astral, gather it in one spot, and with full concentration and intent speak the Charge over it, thus binding it to his Word.

What Charge? Well, the old grimoires are full of them. Some of these can seem rather tedious, but others are striking. My favorite is the one Crowley adapted for his "Preliminary Invocation" for the *Goetia*, and it goes like this:

> Hear Me: and make all Spirits subject unto Me: so that every Spirit of the Firmament and of the Ether: upon the Earth and under the Earth: on dry Land and in the Water: of Whirling Air and of Rushing Fire: and every Spell and Scourge of God may be obedient unto Me.

If done properly—with the spirit standing in one's mind's eye and one's attention fixed upon the words—the actual saying of these words will be physically difficult, as if the wizard were using the action of his jaw to subdue the creature. His tendons will be stiff and hard to move, and he would be tempted to rest halfway through were not the consequences of inattention so catastrophic. After the first pronouncement he may wish to repeat the Charge for the sake of thoroughness, and if it is effective each successive repetition should come easier. Three is usually plenty.

Once it is bound a spirit may be conjured to do magick, or a demon compelled to silence. Any spirit that may be conceived of may be called in this way. Whether its task is to heal, to inspire, to attract or repel, if the wish is definite enough for you to want it, there is a specific spirit that can help. Once called and bound, the spirit's power can be used to energize sigils or impart information, and once the wizard knows the spirit's name, he or she can command it while in a normal waking state. This is especially important when attempting to control a demon. In our neophyte's case, he must simply tell his demon to be still. As often as it speaks he must silence it, until it shrivels from lack of nourishment.

We must be aware of some danger though. By treating our psychic sheaths as if they were composites of so many separate spirits, we make our components truly independent, and must treat them so. If we call them up, we must be sure to dismiss them when we're finished, and we must never neglect habitual banishing and centering. Then our points of view will always be poised, our spirits dependent upon our wills for stability and not the other way around. The superiority of position is everything.

Finally we come to the question of what spirits it is lawful to conjure, and what we may do with them once we have done so. As for the "doing," it would seem better to use magick to change self than circumstances. It is better to evoke sexual attractiveness than to conjure Susan E. Jones into your bed; better to conjure a lucrative talent than a legacy; better to build up a protective aura than to cast spells to kill your neighbor's dog. When you change yourself you have no risk of splashbacks from the outside. When you use magick to change the outside world, the splashbacks are inevitable. Then the question is: Are you quick enough to keep from getting wet?

As for what spirits it is lawful to conjure, it depends on what spirits you have, or want to have, and what it is that you really must do while in this particular body. Or as Crowley was told: "Do what thou wilt shall be the whole of the Law." And: "Thou hast no right but to do thy will." For if "every man and every woman is a star," and we stars take care to keep to our own proper orbits, we will gradually gain a momentum that is cosmic in scope, so the falling becomes joy, every act a sacrament, and the Bride wedded to the Son of the King.

This essay is an adaptation of one first published in *Chaos International* no. 1, East Morton, 1986.

# The Holy Guardian Angel

## A Chaotic Perspective

Ever since the publication of S.L. MacGregor Mathers' translation of *The Book of the Sacred Magic of Abramelin the Mage*, the principle of the Holy Guardian Angel has held a tentative place in Western magickal usage. Although it is an 'entity' often welcomed into the lives of individual magicians, it has had a rather awkward time insinuating itself into specific systems of magickal thought. The relationship between Adept and Angel is such a personal one that it does not take the imposition of symbolism well, preferring to define its own, and as it does it can contradict the received wisdom of any system the Adept might have adopted. Of course systems can be made to adjust but, within a group, individual symbolic modifications can be schismatic and disruptive of discipline. Aleister Crowley is the only mage of renown to have welcomed the Angel gladly, for it meshes perfectly with the cosmic individuality of his own approach.

In pragmatic terms, the magician's conjuration of his or her Angel serves to focus his or her awareness onto a level of attention that is somehow more spiritual, less material than that of mundane experience. The attainment of this height of awareness gives the magician a broad perspective over the various aspects of his (or her) personality—spirits and demons alike—and so he acquires the insight and power needed to dominate them.

This is the dynamic of the procedure. To carry it out as a practical program, the wizard needs to impose symbolic labels onto the different psychic components he will be manipulating. This is because the visualization of sigils, symbols and god-forms and the vibration of spirit names are some of our best tools for manipulating the stuff of the unconscious. We need to be able to call our Angels, and also to see what comes when we do so. What we look for, and how we go about our searches, can depend upon the school of magick to which we belong. But the use of something like the Angel can be found in most every school, even in some rather surprising.

In Christianity, for instance, there is a substantial charismatic faction, thriving in both Roman and Evangelical varieties, wherein devotees conjure the image of the Savior and seek direct contact with Him, especially (in the Roman usage) His Sacred Heart. Both the Roman and the Protestant versions of these movements are viewed somewhat askance by the more established factions of the Faith, most especially because their followers often claim miraculous powers that are more conducive to individual exaltation than institutional. This follows the HGA dynamic perfectly, though naturally the moral and theological stultification intrinsic to the Christian path makes any more than a passing reference to it inappropriate.

The root of this stultification is Jewish monotheism and its associated obsession with sin. It is ironic that Jewish monotheism was also the philosophical foundation of Abramelin's magick and the strong comfort of the book's alleged author, Abraham the Jew of Worms. That the originators of Abramelin's system solved this contradiction is a credit to their genius, and the way they did it tells us much of practical use regardless of our symbolic orientation.

As cosmic speculation, the scheme of Abramelin is almost embarrassingly conventional. Up at the top stands the Lord God Almighty, Creator of the Universe. Then come his Holy Angels, and then creation itself, including ourselves. Mixed in with creation and doing the work of manifestation are the Evil Spirits, ex-Angels who retain their spiritual natures but who in punishment for their rebellion against God are condemned to serve God's Angels and also us humans, His favorites in creation. But because of our mortal natures—our positions as souls trapped in bodies of flesh full of passions and sin—we are not intrinsically above these beings, and if we would use them safely we must first strive to make ourselves superior to them. To Abramelin and Abraham, the way to do this was to fear the Lord and "to wish to live and die in His most Holy Law, and in obedience to Him." In fact, for Abraham the whole of his spiritual support comes from the Lord, with only magickal help coming from his Angel. The Angel's role seems confined to giving information concerning what spirits we have available, the ways they may best be dominated, the ways they may be used once under control, and the ways the magician may keep on close terms with the Lord God, from Whom his power must ultimately derive. The knowledge of the Angel is itself a boon from God, an indication of His infinite mercy for those He made in His Image.

As is well-known, Abramelin prescribed a six-month seclusion as the means by which the aspirant might win this gift, during which time he would devote himself to prayer, study of the scriptures, and constant rereadings of the text of *The Sacred Magic*. Abramelin/Abraham stresses the need to affirm one's humble status as a sinful mortal who can only hope that the Lord's Grace will grant the knowledge of the Holy Angel. The aspirant must be chaste—clean in mind, body and behavior—and he or she[2] must shun any sort of vanity or putting on of airs. Business may be undertaken during the first four months, but always honestly, giving a good value for a fair price, and always refraining from any sort of anger or debauch. The last two months mark an intensification of these austerities. The man must leave his wife and business, and increase his prayer and personal cleanliness and ceremonies of devotion. His only work may be that whose end is charity to his neighbor.

Now in all these ways does the aspirant follow our dynamic of Self-elevation. He raises his intrinsic point of perception and decision (will) so it is above his ambitions, passions, memories, resent-

---

[2] As Abramelin/Abraham grudgingly admits, but only for virgins. For his part, Mathers remarks that he personally knows many women, married and single, who excel in the occult arts.

ments, talents, and all the other personality fragments he normally is immersed within. The austerities put him out of reach of his fragments, and from this distance he can understand and dominate them. To Abraham we do this by the Grace of God, but this may be considered a belief that is true mostly because it works. He looks up to God, and whether God exists as sin-obsessed Yahweh or not, the man will still be removing himself from his mundane involvements and aspiring to whatever sources of power do actually feed our essential Selves.

Once the link with this source has been established and the Adept knows his Angel, the Adept must immediately use his new knowledge and power to bind the evil spirits so they will obey his Word, and so help him work the Sacred Magic for the honor and glory of God, for his own use, and for that of his neighbor.

This, in fact, is an essential dictum, and it confirms our essential premise. For Abraham, if an Adept uses the magic for evil, even after he has the knowledge of his Angel and has dominated the spirits, he will lose the aid of the Angel and the spirits will be free to tear his soul apart at their leisure. By our modern interpretation we might say that by committing a mean or exploitive act we will fall from our exalted perspectives, wallowing in whatever passions we so gratify, and thus we identify ourselves with them and allow them to lead us on to personal and spiritual disaster.

Abramelin/Abraham stresses that the spirits are truly sneaky in their attempts to ensnare the aspirant's soul. At the outset of the aspirant's austerities, he will be visited by a Being of Light who will promise all sorts of powers, but who must be rejected. The powers this Being gives are real enough, for they are those provided by the aspirant's own spirits, but without the backing of his Angel they will overwhelm him. For the same reason Abraham cautions against using any other sort of magick, for instance that practiced by Greek or Egyptian, for though the spirits are real, without the aid of one's Angel one must inevitably be torn apart by them. And even with the Angel, the spirits will continually probe for weak spots. "If they know that a man is inclined unto Vanity and Pride, they will humiliate themselves before him, and push that humility unto excess, and even unto idolatry, and this man will glory herein and become intoxicated with conceit, and the matter will not end without him commanding them some pernicious thing of such nature that ultimately thencefrom will be derived that sin which will make the Man the Slave of the Demon." (pp. 254–255)

The way to avoid this is always to keep the spirits in their place, "for in employing them, if you make unto them the least submission, the slightest prayer or honour, you are rendering yourselves their slaves, and they are in no way submitting to you." From our modern perspective, we can say that this is simply a function of spirit on any given plane. The normal person is on the same plane as his or her personality fragments, and it is characteristic of spirits on the same plane to dissolve and coagulate and mix and separate, much like drops of oil on the surface of water. When our spirits are empowered only by circumstances, hormones and our normal passions and purposes, they seldom become so powerful that they can overwhelm us. But if we empower them magickally, they can become so strong that if we mingle with them they can possess us. To use them safely we must have access to the plane above, wherefrom we may bind them so it sticks. Then they will obey us within the spheres of their power, and only if we give in to them can they threaten our preeminence.

To nail down the essence of the process, then, we might say that we need only have a height we may look up to, and whether we call it the Lord God or Tao, Nuit or Kia is of little consequence. Nor need we see the Angel as any sort of authoritarian superego demanding that we follow conventional morality. Abraham gives the Angel authority only over our use of the spirits and our operation of the magick. The morality comes from the Lord God, the Prophets, and the Law. In the same way, a Taoist could balance the yin and the yang, a Thelemite could do his will, and a Kiaist could ride the shark of her desire, all the while obeying the Angel in matters of magickal practice. Abramelin/Abraham confirms this by telling us that even Turks and Pagans can work the Holy Magic, so long as they affirm the Oneness of God, which Mathers interprets as meaning that both theistic and pantheistic conceptions are acceptable. The aspirant must recognize the existence of some higher plane above his spiritual sheath. The specific tradition that lifts him there is irrelevant.

This stripping the Angel of any moral role has a practical purpose as well as philosophical and theoretical ones, for it keeps any one of our spirits from co-opting the role of Angel and obsessing us with its own particular bias, a real danger if we use a modern short-cut instead of Abramelin's six-month retirement. It allows us to say that the Angel has *no* knowledge except of the various powers we have available to us, *no* power except that which will compel these powers to submission, and *no* authority over us except in the matter of the use of these powers in magick, and which powers we may rightfully evoke. Thus if we meet a being on the astral that tells us it is our Angel, and then in the next breath informs us that if we would advance on the path of power, we must call our mother more often than twice a month, we can legitimately wonder if perhaps our Angel has been co-opted by our spirit of filial obligation, and endeavor to separate one from the other through magickal means.

Once our Angels do thus stand alone, we have available an entity that is far more useful in its way than any generalized bringer of power. The Angel will not bring down power from Heaven, but it will identify powers that can, or parts of your psychic anatomy that you can open so it flows in naturally. It can even suggest powers that you might find useful in the event of a magickal impasse or period of stagnation. On the other hand, if a power is not suitable for your use and you request it anyway, your Angel may find truly creative ways of dissuading you.

I can recall a time when I had reached a stagnant point in my magickal progress and decided it would be amusing to ask my Angel for the power of prescience, just so I could know how the twisted strands of consequence that were my life at the time were apt to line up. It is my custom to write out a ritual in my magickal record before I begin it, so my question for my Angel—"What is the name and symbol for the power of prescience?"—was established before I began. Thus was my intention solid when I banished and separated my bodies for the astral trip.

What I first saw when I stood up on the astral were two men dressed in slacks and sport jackets—middle-aged Caucasians with pot-bellies, crew cuts, wearing white shirts and skinny ties—that is, plainclothes cops. And then in my mind's ear, as clear as anything, I heard them say, "Federal Astral Control Authority. I'm sorry, sir, you can't go up tonight. The planes are closed."

"What?"

The statement was repeated.

So I banished, hard, which seemed to work, after a fashion, for everything was black again. But underneath the black, as if I had just papered them over, were two lumps, and when I poked the film the two Feds broke through.

They weren't fazed in the least, or even angry. "Federal Astral Control Authority," they said. "I'm sorry, sir, you can't go up tonight. The planes are closed." And I knew that if I ignored them and went ahead anyway, these two flatfoots would follow, messing up the trip and maybe even me. And then again, maybe there was such a thing as the Federal Astral Control Authority, and these guys were real. So I said, "Look guys, I think you're just an hallucination, but since you won't leave, I'll make you a deal. Since you're Feds, you naturally know everything, including my phone number, so why don't you just call me up on the phone, and then I'll believe you're real." Remarkably enough, they agreed and left, as if to go call. I waited long enough for them to do so, but heard nothing from my phone, so I banished again and went on up.

As soon as I called my Angel she appeared and told me straight out that if I wanted to have things like that happen regularly, I should go ahead and ask for powers like prescience. I mumbled something dubious so she pressed on to ask if I really wanted prescience, if I had thought out what it would mean to someone as obsessively calculating as myself. I admitted that I hadn't and assured her that it wasn't really necessary, that I could do without it. She let me know she wasn't mad at me, and then I went home.

Now in traditional magick I would have been barred from a knowledge of prescience by some demon from the pit, whom I would have been unable to overcome without the proper initiations, which would have given me either the ability to handle the power or the wisdom not to want it. In my case I got cops, which were probably more effective than any demon could have been. If I'd gotten a demon, I would have tried to overcome it; with cops, I knew better than to fight. The thing about cops is that you can't get rid of them by blasting them, since even if you can hit the first two, they'll keep coming until they get you. You have to use a ruse, which I did, but the impression they made was deep enough to make me quite willing to agree with my Angel's arguments against getting that particular power.

Another point is that my Angel did not deny that the power existed, only asserting that things wouldn't work out if people like me had it. It seemed as if she would have given it if only I had insisted, though I knew that I would totally alienate her if I had, and then I would have had a power I couldn't handle and no help to handle it. So I did what I was told. But there was nothing moral about it, and in no way do I think I would have been a sinner if I had insisted. Not a sinner; just stupid.

Finally we should note that these guardians on the planes had no relation to any symbolic system except the one I use to get along in the mundane world, and by using that glamour they got their point across without confusion. That is, the dynamic of their actions made the consequences of my intended course of action perfectly clear. This reliance on reading energy flow rather than interpreting imagery seems to me to be a distinguishing characteristic of Chaos Magick. The fact that the attainment of one's Angel can be seen in dynamic terms, without reference to symbolism or righteous behavior, implies that it may be a worthy prize for adherents to the Chaos approach. Of course the dynamic we have described requires levels of 'god' down to 'spirit' down to 'matter,' but this need not be a bar, for levels like these are obvious once we look for them. And if some say that the distinction between matter and spirit is an arbitrary one, and false, I will reply that this is so. In essence All is spirit, and what we interpret as matter is spirit also, the crystallization in three dimensions of the will of spirit—its energy—the consequence of "Self-love in complete perspective," serving "its own invincible purpose of ecstasy."

First published in *Chaos International* no. 3, Leeds 1987.

# Astral Projection

## I. Introduction

Astral projection is a convention of contemplation that offers us direct access to our unconscious minds. All that we perceive, all that we think and feel ourselves to be, is influenced by mental processes that operate beneath the surface of awareness. A person who seems most successful may be miserable within; one beset by external troubles may have the psychic competence to transform negative energies into positive and emerge happy and triumphant. Such differences can all be attributed to the way we process our external circumstances, the way we turn raw sense data into mood, thought and action. Or to put it another way, they depend on the powers, complexes, structures, archetypes, spirits, demons and whatever else we wish to call the contents of the unconscious. It is these we may access and manipulate through the technique of astral projection.

The procedure that distinguishes astral projection from regular meditation or yoga is the separation of the "astral body" from the "physical body," and it is through this astral body that we experience what is by definition the astral plane. On this plane we may explore the unconscious as if we were travelers moving through a landscape, with our various mental elements as features or inhabitants of it. This region may be assumed to be infinite, ranging from personal levels to levels that are collective for all humans and even those that comprise the formative forces behind all life—the elements of the Mind of God. But this is conjectural and lies beyond our purpose here. For this essay we will mostly be concerned with the personal level, the elements of which must be under control before any deeper strata may be addressed.

Before we begin, I should clarify what I mean by "unconscious mind." I do not use it to refer to anything necessarily pathological, but merely to those mental mechanisms that operate beneath everyday awareness. I'm no Freudian, and to me the unconscious includes the mental patterns behind reflexes, inclinations, talents, preferences, and emotional responses to circumstances as well as those complexes that could be seen as dysfunctional. The ways we tend to perceive things, the types of relationship we tend to get into, the sorts of job we tend to excel at—all these will have an unconscious component and so may be made available for inspection and manipulation during astral projections. I don't see that these complexes become unconscious because we're afraid of them or because of any psychic censor, but simply because once we assimilate a routine as a response to circumstances, it acquires its own identity and sinks down to the level of reflex, where it can no longer be easily recalled. Of course we experience the results of their operation, but these manifestations only tell us the reflexes are there. They do not make them available for inspection or manipulation. In fact, during their manifestation it will generally be quite impossible to work with them, for they literally possess us at these times, forcing us to experience our situations in terms of the necessities of their operation, without regard for logical standards of truth. But their recall can be accomplished if we work at it, either through introspection, hypnotherapy, psychotherapy, or astral projection. And only astral projection allows us to accomplish this recall directly and deliberately so that we meet the unconscious element face-to-face. Once we see it thus stark before us—without any interface of professional intervention to serve as a sanitary barrier—we may directly confront it and compel it to conform to our wills. Any indirect way of attempting this sort of manipulation, for instance by simply conjuring to produce the desired effect, will be uncertain compared to astral working. During an astral confrontation with an unconscious complex, we will invariably gain some insight into its origins and operations, insight that will help us in our overall understanding of our personalities, even if our magick alone is sufficient to control it.

## II. The Astral Body and Its Separation

As I remarked at the beginning, the essence of astral projection is the separation of the astral body from the physical body, then traveling in that body through the astral space thus revealed. But in order to do this we must first define and develop our astral bodies. Aleister Crowley, whose instructions in *Magick in Theory and Practice* served as the basis for my own astral researches, states that the way to develop the astral body is to separate it from the physical and then exercise it by using it for astral explorations. As he put it: "Develop your Body of Light until it is just as real to you as your other body." (p. 146) We must use it to practice traveling to whichever symbols we recognize as significant, and to operate whatever rituals and conjurations we need to exploit them. It is our vehicle for exploring the subtle planes, and we must educate it in all aspects of this work.

The way Crowley suggests separating your bodies is by closing your eyes and imagining a shape resembling your own standing in front of you. This you define as your astral body, and to begin the projection you transfer your point of view into it so that you see with its eyes, hear with its ears, and stand on its feet. Crowley remarks that you should then look around to see the objects in the room through these eyes, though of course this vision must be of the objects' astral analogues, rather than their physical natures. Crowley tells us that we shouldn't dismiss our results as the mere revelation of "subconscious memory," that "the time to test that is later on." (p. 147) But perhaps we should admit to that, and then go on to say that since it is our unconscious impression of things that we wish to examine, that is all we *should* want. But then I don't want to get all that philosophical here, so we'll move right along.

It is probably best for the novice to begin his or her astral practices by separating bodies as Crowley describes, but there are other methods as well. The Golden Dawn method involved visualizing a symbol of the power one wished to explore, then stepping astrally through it into the plane itself, using the "Sign of the Enterer" (perhaps even physically) to project oneself through the symbol, and then once through assuming for a moment the "Sign of Silence."[3] Speaking of a projection through the tattwic symbol of Earth (it happens to be a yellow square) in volume four of his *Golden Dawn*, Israel Regardie remarks that once through, the dominant impression "should be a strong sense of being *within* the element." (p. 16) The traveler should have a direct impression of the nature of the element, a feeling of the essence of the thing.

For myself, I have a word of power that enables me to somersault out of my physical body and stand up on the astral—which appears as a region just *above* that where my physical body sits. It is featureless, meaning that I am unable to examine the objects in the room, and remains so until I invoke something into it. Before I do this I generally use another word that causes me to rise up to a considerable height above the physical realm, this to avoid accidental mixing.

Crowley also suggests rising before doing any invoking, though he apparently did it simply by willing the ascent, rather than by using a word of power. According to Crowley, at a certain point the traveler will begin to see entities and landscapes. They are not as solid as material objects, but are more so than mental images—"they seem to lie between the two." (p. 146) For my part, it's been years since I've seen anything I haven't called up. This might mean I've done a pretty thorough job of housecleaning, or maybe that I'm just getting boring in my old age.

---

[3] With the Sign of the Enterer, also called Horus, the magician porjects his energy by taking one step forward as he dips his head and extends his arms straight ahead, his fingers pointing to the place to be penetrated or the object to be charged. With the Sign of Silence, also called Harpocrates, the magician pulls his energy back in on itself by standing erect as he either puts his fingers to his lips, or his thumb in his mouth.

With both these gestures, an awareness of the motion involved in making it is as important as awareness of the posture itself.

There is, of course, no right or wrong here, except with regard to the right way of maintaining psychic integrity. And this brings us to two critical topics: reuniting our bodies, and our relations with the spirits. The first I will use to close this section; the second will take up the next section.

To get onto the astral, we separate our astral bodies from our physical bodies. Then we travel in the astral bodies, leaving the physical behind. To return to normal, we must bring the astral body back into the physical body and fix it there so it sticks. To do this you must return your astral body to where you left the physical, taking care to go back in reverse order over the same astral landscape you traveled on the way out. Once back at your point of departure, you should move your astral body back into your physical body so that the features of their respective anatomies coincide—astral fingers matching physical fingers, astral feet matching physical feet, astral head matching physical head, and so on. Then you should tense all your muscles at once, bring your forefinger to your lips in the sign of Harpocrates, and then—**in one instant**—wake up!

Crowley stresses that it is imperative that the traveler do this at the end of each experiment, even the novice who is positive that he or she never got his or her bodies separated to begin with. To neglect this is to allow the astral body to wander off on its own, where it can be "attacked and obsessed." (p.147) This will result in symptoms ranging from headaches and bad dreams to hysterical paralysis and insanity. In short, you will be left all at loose ends, and permanent degradation of your aura will be the inevitable result if you continue the practice.

Now always being one to follow good advice, I have never tested Crowley's procedure by ignoring it, and so I can't give much in the way of first-hand experience. But I did once meet a woman who told me that she had once practiced astral projection without bothering to reunite, simply going to bed as soon as she tired. And then one morning she awoke with a paralyzed arm, which took two or three days to regain its function. For my own part, I can say that however prosaic I may feel at the end of a trip just before reuniting, the act of reunion does seem to produce a quantum jump in alertness. I may have felt normal just before, but the way I felt afterwards confirmed that I had not been.

# III. Managing Spirits

To say that the entities, complexes, or tangles of aether that make up our unconscious minds are "spirits" is, I admit, a convention, but it is one that is effective, so I'll be using it here. It's just that when we treat them as spirits in the sorcerous sense, they can be managed using the techniques of sorcery, and so it seems prudent to do so, even when it is obvious just from their astral appearance that they are not. It's all well and good to try to discover what they "really" are, but as Frater U D pointed out in his "Models of Magic"[4], all we'll get if we do so is another model. It seems to me that a reliance on convention is the best way out of this conundrum, just so long as we focus on the dynamic of what happens rather than the labels we stick on the components that make up the event.

Given the use of the spirit convention, then, what we do when we astrally project is enter the realm of spirits and meet them one-on-one. By doing so we win the opportunity to manipulate them, but we also make ourselves available to be manipulated by them. To maintain psychic integrity, it is imperative that we always keep the upper hand. Three considerations are of prime importance: keeping the spirits separate from ourselves, ascertaining their true natures, and binding them to obedience.

Keeping the spirits separate from ourselves is a matter of keeping a distance both "spatially" and emotionally, and using banishing to purge our auras both before and after working. Keeping a distance means you should never allow their astral forms to mix with your own, and you should never allow yourself to become too familiar with them. When we project we are entering their territory, and by calling up specific ones, we are meeting

---

[4] In *Chaos International* no. 9.

them in an energized state. So we must be sure that we are always the masters, and they the servants. This implies the calm assumption of authority. The imperious pose of an autocrat or a bully they would perceive as symptomatic of an inner fear, to be exploited at leisure, while to set them up as "holy beings" would be to reverse roles with them and welcome obsession by them.

Banishing, on the other hand, is simply a way to start clean and finish clean, though it may also be needful as a defense during the projection itself. A full banishing is vital before the separation of bodies and just before their reunion. One should also use a brief sort of banishing after one licenses an invoked spirit to depart, just to make sure it really goes. This could be anything from a pentagram drawn with one's astral dagger to the vibration of an appropriate word of power. In all these things experience will provide the tools, if only one's progress be deliberate and persistent.

More subtle than any attempts by the entities to invade our astral persons is the potential for deception on their part. Crowley warns us that every spirit we meet—from the lowest to the highest—will try to persuade us that it is more important than it is. On the most fundamental level, there is the human tendency to judge a spirit's importance or validity by how vivid one's vision of it might be. There can be no greater error, simply because the intensity of the vision only indicates how much energy it has behind it, and nothing else. Thus an adolescent's vision of his or her sexual anxiety might be utterly awesome, terrible to behold, but ripe for deflation by one good roll in the hay. The importance of this consideration can be illustrated by any number of visionary incidents from the Jewish and Christian canons—from Ezekiel's vision of the Chariot of God to Saul's encounter on the road to Damascus. In each case the vision was reported to be utterly stunning, but even if we grant the sincerity of the witness, how much of the vision was the product of the visionary's own abreacted despair (in the case of Ezekiel), or energy sent by others through that type of conjuring known as prayer (in the case of Saul)? If Saul was actually reacting to energy sent by the Nazarenes he was persecuting, perhaps we could conclude that the last twenty centuries of vexing nightmare were set in motion not by a rocking cradle, but instead by the fulminating self-righteousness of a self-loathing prig.

With such potentially disastrous consequences, we can see the importance of knowing precisely what a spirit represents before we invest it with our credibility. In some ways, of course, it is impossible to be absolutely sure. As Crowley put it, "the authentic Nakhiel is indistinguishable from the image of the Magician's private idea of Nakhiel." (p. 253) The more power we have, the more readily the astral will create spirits to satisfy our wants. Of course one who has assimilated the Rosicrucian system will have an image of the intelligence of the Sun within his or her unconscious, and so it must have an astral appearance. The essential thing is to keep it true to what an intelligence of the Sun should be, and not let it inflate itself into something demonic. After all, the first things we are likely to meet once we start exploring our unconscious minds are spirits representing our own self-importance, and if they are able to co-opt legitimate spirits, and thus claim our credibility and support, they will grow until they swallow us whole.

In his *Ritual Magic in England*, Francis King offers an illustration of this process when he writes of the activities of the Stella Matutina, the most magickally oriented fragment of the Golden Dawn to survive after the departure of W.B. Yeats and Annie Horniman. Within the Stella Matutina was a group of three "adepts" who indulged in an ongoing series of astral visits to an organization of "Hidden Masters." These visions were supposed to result in great initiations of earthshaking import, but concluded in nothing more than the mental breakdown of the participants. Of the three members of the group, one died in a mental hospital while the leader, a Miss Stoddart, "became a sort of jingoistic protofascist." She started writing a column for *The Patriot* under the name "Inquire Within," convinced that all magickal orders including the Stella Matutina were part of a Jewish conspiracy for world domination, a conspiracy that included, among others, the German General Staff! Paranoia, once it begins, can have no natural limits.

King points out that a prime cause of this astral extravagance was an uncritical acceptance of the truth of the visions received.

Mathers and Crowley both stressed that it was necessary to impose a symbolic discipline onto one's visions, and this was best done by imposing an overriding symbolic scheme, map of power, or "anatomy of the body of God" onto one's symbolic universe. For Mathers and Crowley, this was the Tree of Life of the Hermetic Qabalah with its ten Sephiroth and the 22 paths between them. A Taoist, on the other hand, would have his own scheme based on the combinations of yin and yang, a Roman Catholic would have the communion of Saints, and so on. Crowley insisted that the symbolic components of each such system could be made to fit on the Tree, though at times the disinterested observer has to suspect he was stretching it.

In any event, before beginning a projection, one should choose a specific symbol to explore and take care to travel to its specific locale. Once on the astral, you could begin your invocation of the symbol by using the Sign of the Rending of the Veil[5] to open a door emblazoned with it, and using the opposite gesture immediately to close it once you had stepped through. If one's system is based on Hermetic Qabalah, one should then invoke with the appropriate god-name and pentagram and hexagram until a spirit-guide appears. This guide should be dressed in the colors of the Sephirah appropriate to the symbol, and it should be tested by assuming the grade signs of the Sephirah and by asking if it comes in the name of the Sephirah's god-name. Legitimate spirits will grow stronger; impostors will disintegrate. And the same goes for any other spirits one meets as one travels around the symbol.

Another classic way to assert authority is to assume the form of the god who has dominion over the symbol in question. The god-form is the traditional representation of the power the god represents, an ideal shape, while the spirits one meets on the astral are actual entities with their own particular reasons for being, and thus their own special independence. Thus assuming god-forms is not risky like letting a spirit occupy your aura is risky. Assuming god-

---

[5] Make it by holding your hands out in front of you back-to-back, and then open your arms as if you were prying open double doors. Always follow it with the closing gesture, once you have gone through.

forms is invocation. Letting a spirit occupy your aura is an invitation to obsession.

Of course the problem with all of this is that it is only appropriate for those who are willing to program their unconscious minds with a specific symbolic tradition. In the case of the Golden Dawn, it meant that every unit of meaning one wished to investigate first had to be attributed to a specific location on the Tree of Life, for otherwise one would have no standard symbolism against which to check the vision. This is obviously unacceptable to those who reject the Neoplatonic assumptions at the root of the Qabalistic ontology, or even to those like myself who can accept aspects of the Neoplatonism but find the Tree of Life too limited to describe the complexities of unconscious architecture and its connection to the undifferentiated Absolute. Our unconscious minds are each unique to ourselves and to explore them with competence we must do so without a map. Instead, we must draw the map ourselves as we probe into them, naming each location or inhabitant with our own special names as we find them.

But still the risk of self-inflation and deception remains, and in any case we have to have the ability to call what we want. And so we need a way to invoke specific entities and to check our visions of them.

The solution I have adopted is a variation on Austin Spare's elementary method of conjuring, this applied to the Golden Dawn procedure for astral projection. To meet any specific spirit on the astral, you can begin your preparations by defining its function in a brief sentence. Then you should eliminate the duplicate letters so there is only one of each, and from these design a monogram. You should begin to fill this sigil with energy, visualizing it whenever you have free belief that you've released by dismembering passions via the Neither-Neither principle. It shouldn't take much to vivify such a sigil for astral purposes; a few commutes in traffic and a spat with your pelvic affiliate should be enough, much less than what you would require to spawn a physical event. When you go onto the astral you are entering the spirits' own territory, not requiring them to act in yours, so the energy requirements are much lower.

Once you have energized your sigil, you should begin to use it as a means for automatic drawing, this as a way of designing a sacred letter to represent the spirit in question. To do this simply doodle aimlessly while staring at the sigil—until you recognize a shape or arrangement of lines that appears to represent the power dynamic the spirit controls. This you should abstract into a discrete character. Once you have one that looks appropriate, you should confirm it with a series of divinations with whatever oracle you find reliable. Finally, you can construct a mantra by means of a phonic degradation of the sentence that defines your spirit (and which you used to construct the sigil). This technique is described by Ray Sherwin in his *Book of Results* and Peter J. Carroll in *Liber Null*, and consists of removing duplicate letters and rearranging syllables to produce an appropriately "barbarous" name of evocation. Such a mantra could also serve as a name for the spirit, or perhaps you'll find that other methods do better. For myself, I first started by constructing names from Crowley's "Order and Value of the English Alphabet," then by receiving them directly from my Holy Guardian Angel, who told me her name after I succeeded in invoking her. However you do it, names are necessary. You need to have a name to address the spirit when you bind it. You'll also need one to call the spirit up or silence it while in normal consciousness, either to obtain its assistance or to be rid of it. An important qualification, however, is that this needs to be a "barbarous name" instead of a description in English of what you think the spirit represents. English descriptions come from consciousness, and that can be limiting. Better to give it a 'proper' nonsense name, and let it define its own identity.

In any case, between the mantra, the alphabetic sigil and the sacred letter, you should have enough symbolism to call up and test the spirit in question, allowing you to proceed in using Crowley's technique just described, or any convenient variation thereof. That is, use the sigil or go through a sigil-marked door to enter the spirit's realm, and call it with the mantra, then use the mantra with the sigil and sacred letter to test what comes. Impostors will disintegrate where true spirits will grow stronger, perhaps so strong that the confrontation becomes unpleasant, for instance if the spirit is a demon whose greatest stimulus to growth was some personal weakness or immaturity.

But this is not to say this method is free of technical difficulties. In fact, in practice it is incredibly awkward. Each spirit requires a separate sigil to call it up; it is quite impossible to ascertain the true nature of spirits you might meet "by chance" during projections; and hence there is no way to map the results of deliberately unfocused explorations of the astral landscape. Frankly, if we are to explore the astral without a traditional map like the Tree of Life, we need a guide. For this reason, and not out of any aspiration toward the Transcendent Highest, I have frequently reiterated the need to acquire the Knowledge and Conversation of the Holy Guardian Angel, that entity which was introduced into the English magickal tradition by *The Book of the Sacred Magic of Abramelin the Mage*, translated by S.L. MacGregor Mathers.

Now dogmatic Chaoists might say that my reiteration in this case has been done *ad nauseam*, but like any ideologues, dogmatic Chaoists are invariably ignorant, unlike the enlightened, open-minded people reading this essay. And being open-minded myself, I try to keep my practical assumptions concerning the HGA as non-dogmatic as possible, even though my personal feelings about it do tend toward the Neoplatonic. But I'm trying to be relentlessly practical here, so I'll confess that logically there's no way to know whether one's conjuration of the Angel calls down a preexistent spirit from the highest aspects of personality (as Crowley and I would have it), or whether we manufacture the Angel out of unformed psychic stuff through the months-long reiteration of the conjuration. Only a truly objective perspective could tell us which alternative is correct, a perspective that cannot exist, or not in this universe anyway.

Regardless of where we believe it comes from, the most relentlessly practical way to look at the HGA is as a sort of personnel director, executive secretary or foreman who has knowledge of and authority over all the elements of one's spiritual swarm, *but no other function at all*. Thus it can tell you what spirits are responsible for a given function, what their names are, how to evoke them, and whether it would be wise for you to evoke them, but not if you would still be holy if you bought a new car. By thus focusing the Angel's operation, we make it much more powerful than any generalized bringer of good advice, and we also keep it from being contaminated by spirits with axes of their own to grind which might wish to co-opt the authority of the Angel in order to sharpen them. Incidentally, this restriction of the Angel's function is entirely in accord with Abramelin's treatment of it. For him the good advice came from the Lord God, the Prophets and the Law, with the Angel having authority only over the spirits and how we might properly use them.

The way to become acquainted with one's Angel was originally the six-month seclusion prescribed by Abramelin the Mage. A more modern version is the ten months of increasingly frequent repetitions of *Liber Samekh* suggested by Aleister Crowley. But in fact the method of using sigils and sacred letters is also effective, and takes less time, though it may require several weeks of filling your sigil with free belief before your Angel appears in your astral vision. And I should add that after I'd met my Angel by using this method, I used several dozen repetitions of *Samekh* to cement the relationship. However you do it, the crux is learning the Angel's name, for then you may call it with ease—whether to advise you in the details of your spiritual working or to help you manage some astral situation that is in danger of getting out of hand.

To close this section on managing spirits, I would emphasize that before you work with any spirit, from the lowest demon to your Holy Angel, it is necessary to bind it to your will. The way to do this is to collect it in front of you within your astral vision and then recite a ritual charge over it. Traditional charges from the old grimoires work very well here, but whether you use one of them or not, the charge you do use should be long enough that its recitation is something of a production. To simply say "Obey me in all things!" would be an incompetent's cop-out, and you can be sure it would be totally ineffective. For myself, I use the charge Crowley adapted for his "Preliminary Invocation" for the *Goetia*, which reads:

> Hear Me; and make all Spirits subject unto Me: so that every Spirit of the Firmament and of the Ether: upon the Earth and under the Earth: on dry Land and in the Water: of Whirling Air, and of Rushing Fire: and every Spell and Scourge of God may be obedient unto Me.

Said with full concentration and intent, these words will be difficult to pronounce, as if the motion of your jaw were what was doing the binding. You should repeat the charge until its pronouncement becomes easy, at which point you can be sure the spirit will obey you within the limits of its power, if only you have the presence of mind to command its obedience.

# IV. Preparations for Projection

Astral projection, though one of the easier occult practices, is still not something you can just sit down and do without preparation. Two types of preliminary work need to be attended to: work on mental readiness, and work on the procedures and props that support the projection itself.

The most basic sort of mental preparation is a substantial period of regular meditation, for instance the type of raja yoga that Crowley offers in Part One of his *Book Four*. You need to acquire at least a simple posture for asana so your body won't distract you, familiarity with pranayama so your breathing becomes automatic, and you need to practice dharana to increase your ability to concentrate, to attend to the matter at hand without the intrusion of distracting thoughts. This last is especially important if you decide to vivify your astral visions with sacraments such as cannabis, which surely does make them brighter and sharper, though at some cost to mental control.

A purely mental aid to visualization was suggested by Mathers in his introduction to *The Book of the Sacred Magic of Abramelin the Mage*, and with its perfection may come the power of clairvoyance.

> This thought-vision is exercised almost unconsciously by everyone in thinking of either a place, person, or thing, which they know well; immediately, coincident with the thought, the image springs before the mental sight; and it is but the conscious and voluntary development of this which is the basis of what is commonly called clairvoyance. (p. xxvii)

To apply this in practice, simply translate every possible thought into visual form. If you remind yourself that you have to meet Fred for tea, at the same time force yourself to visualize the shop wherein you'll be taking it, Fred's face and likely mode of dress, which table you'll likely sit at, and so on. After a few weeks of this, visual thinking should come much more easily, perhaps even supplanting your verbal thought-stream for long periods of time. The truly dedicated may find that the application of Crowley's *Liber III vel Jugorum* will greatly intensify the process.[6]

---

[6] *Liber III* is a discipline which consists of taking oaths, for specific periods of time, forbidding specific arbitrary actions: physical acts, the utterance of certain words, the thinking of certain thoughts. One could forbid the touching of one's face with one's left hand for a week, speaking the word "of" for two weeks, or thinking about politics in the month before a presidential election. Since it is certain that such an oath will be violated, a punishment must be specified for each and every infraction, and the only one that is practical to use frequently is physical pain. Crowley suggested slashing the wrist with a straight razor, but that's just sick. A pin, concealed in a hem, can be good to stick your leg with; you can fit a thick rubber band around your wrist and give yourself a good snap; or you can just bite your thumb.

An essential point here is that the things you deny yourself must be innocuous. If they had any emotional or moral value—for instance if you forbade yourself thinking about how you were bullied in school and the teachers didn't care—that would be repression, which all psychiatrists agree is a sure route to mental and physical illness. It is better to build up your will on denials that are utterly arbitrary, and then use it to do formal evocations of the demons at the

*Liber III* practiced as a general discipline is also a superb way to develop the strength of will that will guarantee superiority over any recalcitrant spirits or demons you might meet on the astral. Since you are going to their realm, it is imperative that you be stronger than they are if you are to be sure that you'll return with your psychic equipment intact.

Physical preparations for astral projection consist of the things you have to do and use to make it work. The most obvious requirement is that you must ensure that you will not be disturbed during the projection. Even the threat of a disruption will make it difficult to go into trance, and a ringing phone or a demand for attention by animal or human housemates can put one at loose ends, indeed. The obvious solution is to live alone in the country without a phone, though working late at night with sympathetic housemates fast asleep is almost as suitable.

Hardly less important than physical security is the need to keep your overall astral progress at least minimally coherent, a goal best accomplished by making a careful record of all your astral work. A record is essential simply to keep track of the various spirits you encounter—their names, functions and symbols—and to note down how successful your dealings with them turn out to be. Astral work is a lifetime thing, and to expect memory or casual notes to keep track of its progress is to guarantee either its discontinuation or its culmination in confusion.

Once these matters of organization have been settled, the question of mind-altering substances needs to be addressed. The most accessible of these are the incenses, and in my experience incense of Abramelin is superb for astral work. According to *The Sacred Magic*, it is a compound of four parts frankincense, two parts storax, and one part lign aloes, "and not being able to get this wood you shall take that of cedar, or of rose, or of citron, or any other odoriferous wood." (p. 77) But there is a problem as to what exactly is meant by storax, in that there are two very different sub-

---

source of such obsessions, thus dealing with them in a straightforward magickal fashion.

stances that go by that name. What I use is sold as "estoraque" in the Santería botanicas. It is a granular resin that looks like a very crude sort of benzoin, with an odor that is a sort of sweet, mild, distinctive muskiness—it seems like I should be able to place it, but I can't. But to breathe its fumes when it's heated does bring on a certain sense of dissociation, and it seems to enhance the sedative effect of the frankincense. Benzoin doesn't do this, and benzoin also smells much sweeter and stronger. Even so, I think this is probably what Abramelin had in mind, since Mrs. M. Grieve's *Modern Herbal* remarks that the solid storax of the ancients was probably *Styrax officinale*. Both Sumatran and Siamese benzoin are from the genus *Styrax*, and all are from the family *Styraceae*.

The other thing called storax comes from the plant *Liquidambar orientalis* of the family *Hamamelaceae* and is sold in the trade as "Storax Praep." It is a liquid about the consistency of molasses and is archetypically sticky, making me think it would be impossible to mix with any but the best-cured frankincense. Also, when it is heated it puts off fumes that seem quite irritating to the sinuses, or to my sinuses, anyway. So I stick with the estoraque.

The less accessible mind-altering substances are, of course, those that are illegal. Marijuana and non-opiated hashish, *in very low doses*, can be very helpful to visualization on the astral, and also can help one to disregard one's physical body, though of course they make concentration more difficult. But if the dosage is too high, one can become so euphoric that it becomes impossible to maintain control, or even coherence of vision. And this question of dosage is tricky, since one can smoke a quantity that seems perfectly manageable in normal consciousness, then go onto the astral and find one has taken too much. Less is more, personal experience is the best guide, and don't hesitate to banish and abort the journey if you find you have taken too much.

Psychedelics like LSD and psilocybin are unsuited for astral work. They make one too aware of one's body to really get out of it.

As for physical props like candles, robes and so on, I would remark that candles are best for lighting, giving enough to visualize by without drawing any attention to their presence. Robing and so on is necessary if you need it, but not otherwise. For my part, I just dab a bit of oil of Abramelin[7] onto each of my chakras while I vibrate their names. I'm not sure if the oil has a psychotropic effect or not, but if it does it's much more subtle than that of the incense, making me think its benefit is mostly psychological. But given, of course, that everything you meet on the astral is an aspect of psyche, what else is there?

# V. Astral Strategies

One of the best ways to avoid being seduced by the delusional aspects of the astral is to have a practical reason for each journey up. If you go up just to wander around searching of enlightenment and amusement, self-deception is almost inevitable. But if you have a specific intention each time, you'll have enough to occupy yourself and hence be less open to distractions. And there is plenty to do. There are demons to be analyzed, named and bound, positive powers to be defined, enhanced and consulted, chakras to penetrate, energy from legitimate sources of resentment to be redirected, primal reflexes to be disconnected. This is not to say that one should map out a program beforehand and then follow it to the letter. Much of what you can accomplish depends on the personal power and control you can accumulate as you go along, and the spontaneous discoveries you make as you do so. But in my experience it all (or something like it all) needs to be done if one's personality is to become a tool for will rather than a burden on it, the vehicle rather than the driver.

One of the very first things neophyte astral travelers should do is identify, name and bind their most flagrant demons. These are the spirits most likely to make the magician miserable or get him or her killed, all the more so since the use of a magickal discipline

---

[7] For oil of Abramelin, combine four parts oil of cinnamon, two parts oil of myrrh, one part oil of galangal, and three and one half parts olive oil.

to accumulate power will mean the demons have that much more to draw on for their benefit and the magician's peril.

Generally speaking, demons are acquired during childhood and adolescence. This explains both their deeply engrained nature and also the childish behavior one tends to exhibit while possessed by them. If, during childhood, our sense of self-worth is assaulted in a specific way, we will perforce develop a specific routine to counter the assaults—one suited to the physical and emotional maturity of a child. As we grow older we will likely transcend the need for this routine; our circumstances will change and we will find more subtle ways to deal with stress. But the original routine will remain deep within our psyches. It will fill our minds with its childish voice whenever circumstances call it up, and if we break down and act on its imprecations, we will make messes of our situations, since our behavior will be inherently immature.

One point should be stressed: all negative or aggressive thought and feeling should not be considered demonic. Much of it may be perfectly legitimate responses to circumstances, and even if it isn't prudent to act upon its advice, it's not something to stifle, but rather to transform. We'll be getting to this transforming toward the end of this section. Demons, on the other hand, tend to pop up on their own under totally inappropriate circumstances, often during periods of mild stress or uncertainty when patience or mere anxiety, irritation or mild exasperation would be more suitable. But a demon will manifest here as panic, rage, or an ardent denunciation of the circumstances. Any objective observer would say that a person displaying such behavior was possessed, though of course the person in thrall to the demon will think that he or she is perfectly justified. The reason for this is that during the attack his or her point of view will be occupied by the demon, and so all thinking and perception will be organized according to its standards. After the attack has run its course, the person may consider that his or her behavior had been unreasonable. If he or she then realizes that this unreasonableness follows a consistent pattern, he or she may decide that something needs to be done. But whatever plan is chosen, it will have to be executed while the demon is in a quiet state. To try to stifle it as it manifests is both hopeless and danger-ous to body and mind. Thus the advantage of astral projection, which allows the person to go into its lair while it sleeps and bind it before it entirely awakes.

The binding of the demon, once it is undertaken, should require no more than an hour's work. Calling them up is easy since, as Crowley tells us, "they are always calling you." Merely designing the sigil, sacred letter and mantra should be enough to ensure its appearance. The only problem is likely to come when the demon is in front of you but not yet bound, and at no other time is it quite so necessary to keep a spirit spatially separate from your astral form. If you have properly evoked it, you should at this point have a clear intuitive picture of the demon's origin and reason for being. And since it is (after all) a demon, this insight will be notably unpleasant. It may even be that some childhood weakness or irre-sponsibility on your part contributed to the demon's formation, and such faults must be acknowledged and accepted if the demon is to be bound successfully. In any event, the confrontation will be no occasion for any sort of self-deception, and the deeper your under-standing of the demon's dynamic, the more complete will be your ultimate dominion over it.

Less malignant than demons but requiring a similar treatment are trains of thought or memory that are annoying and serve no purpose. A good example would be thoughts of people who used to be friends but aren't anymore. Here you should simply define that person's place in your mind as a spirit and bind it, then command its silence whenever thoughts of that person pop into your mind.

But this process should be distinguished from what is required to deal with any anger or resentment toward the person who is no longer a friend. This cannot simply be shut off, but must be trans-formed into something useful. To stifle it would be repression, which Freud, Jung, Reich and all the rest have quite rightly identi-fied as a source of ills both mental and physical. To silence a demon is to acknowledge some hurt from the past even as you keep your immature response to that hurt from stealing the power you have now to distort your present situation. But if the hurt is here and now, it has its own power that must be worked with as such and not merely stifled or swept to one side. The best solution I have found for this is to synthesize a spirit whose sole function is to transform that energy into something you can use, from the power to paint better pictures to the power to attract more customers to your auto repair business. And it isn't just anger at faithless friends that can be used here. In my "Discipline of Demons" in *Chaos International* no. 10, I gave the example of transforming anger at the civil state into literary creativity. Since then I've bound spirits to transform lust of result into the power to see into the essence of any situation, impatience into magickal power, and resentment at being treated with less than due consideration into personal power. (I distinguish between magickal and personal power by regarding the first as the ability to apply energy according to will, and the second as the quantity of energy available to be applied. The first is like the power of one's automobile engine, while the second is like the amount of gasoline in the tank.)

Now the reader here may remark that my purposes here all tend toward self-development rather than practical results, but this focus may be dismissed as my own predilection rather than the one true way to do it. I have a friend who used this method to transform anger at a former associate into more orders for the firm he owns, and it worked very well indeed, considering New England's depressed economy at the time. In this as in all things, *do your own research*. I'm only making suggestions.

In all these cases it is naturally easier if one has the assistance of a Holy Guardian Angel to call up specific spirits and give their names, though I suppose it would be possible to do it with alphabetic sigils, sacred letters, mantras and so on. But I have no idea how I could do this work if I had programmed myself with Rosicrucian symbolism. I wouldn't even know where to begin.

One last astral strategy that I should mention is the disconnection of primal reflexes. I stumbled onto this when I got the flash that one of the reasons that we age is because we expect to. This expectation causes a sort of black depression which is corrosive to physical integrity, just like any other stress such as overwork, malnourishment, sickness, etc. So it seemed that to remove this expectation of aging would at least help slow the process down. When I went onto the astral and inquired of my Angel as to the wisdom of this enterprise, I was taken immediately to a great height wherein there were about a dozen marble pavilions, each of which (I was told) contained the mechanism for a reflex like the expectation of aging. I was told that I could only address the others when I had the power to independently discern their existence, and then was taken to the one that concerned aging, which contained an iron bar glowing red-hot. As soon as I learned its name and bound it with the charge, the glow ceased, and I have not had to deal with it since. Nor have I since had any thoughts of inevitable decay that have lasted longer than twenty seconds. That is, if one occurs it seems as if it blows a fuse and immediately loses power. Of course I am still of an age where my body doesn't tend to remind me of such things; I will be more impressed if I still possess this detachment thirty years hence. But even if my original assumption is wrong, I can still think of no reason to have kept that bit of reflexive thinking, and lots of reasons to be done with it.

In subsequent experiments I have tried to disconnect the reflex that causes me to find and maintain my level of "rank" in interpersonal situations, and that which causes me to take my dreams seriously, this with the intent of gaining the ability to manipulate them in the mode of Carlos Castaneda. In the first case my original intent was to gain the ability to better sink into the background in social situations, but I found it had quite the opposite effect. Two days after the projection I found myself in conversation with the supervisor at my place of employment. Instead of automatically deferring to his rank, I allowed my sense of the situation to determine my manner towards him. Before I knew it we had agreed that American culture was going to hell, that there was no way an educational establishment (like the one wherein we worked) could counter the mind-killing influence of television, and that it was impossible for him to focus on administering the petty discipline it was his job to deal out and still preserve the fine edge of his intellect. I even told him that the best way to learn to read well was to do it while locked in jail with a pile of trash fiction, and that for me it had taken six weeks. Before I knew it, he was signing me up for about quadruple the number of hours I had previously been working, hours I definitely needed to keep the wolf from my door. The effort at dream work was not successful at all. They seem to be more vivid and coherent than ever, displaying episodes that I perceive to be reality even at their most bizarre. Further research is obviously indicated.

## VI. Astral Authenticity

The question of whether what we deal with on the astral is real, or if it's just fantasy, is answerable only by the effects we are able to produce by manipulating it. It's true enough that what we work with is "only imaginary," but then imagination is the interface between waking awareness and the unconscious. The unconscious can impose its contents on waking awareness through imagination, and by acquiring astral competence we can return the favor. By your results you will know just how competent you are.

The classic anecdote concerning astral ontology was written by Aleister Crowley at the beginning of Chapter XVIII of *Magick in Theory and Practice*. This is the story of the two Americans on a train, one of whom was "carrying a basket of unusual shape." The other was curious and inquired as to its contents. A mongoose, he was told. What was a mongoose, he asked. An animal that eats snakes. So why did the man with the basket want that? Because his brother saw snakes. But to this the enquirer protested that those were not *real* snakes. "Sure," said the man with the basket, "but this mongoose ain't real either."

The sole criterion for the "reality" of the imaginary mongoose was whether it could dispose of the imaginary snakes. The snakes might not be flesh and blood, but still they were able to torment the man's brother in his delirium. To dispose of them would be to relieve a real torment, and so the means of disposal would have a reality of its own. Thus if our astral work is effective at managing our mental content, it is real. Otherwise it is only inconsequential self-glorification, self-titillation, or some similar indulgence or pathology.

Of course this is the same criterion for determining the effectiveness of any magickal work, but for myself, I tend to hold my astral efforts to a higher standard than the magick I do to bring about a physical event. With results magick there are always questions of how ready the situation is for what we want to have happen. Perhaps the magick is accomplishing the work it needs to, but is doing this by making the circumstances riper, rather than by actualizing the climactic event. Of course it has been said that to obtain a large result, one should break it up into small increments and attack it in stages, but this assumes that we know beforehand the best steps to take to arrive at the conclusion we desire. It may be better to conjure for the distant goal from the start, acting on the assumption that we thus pressure Fate to actualize whatever small steps are required. Then after we do our magick we should only take care to respond to any small coincidences that tend toward the ultimate goal, and not count it as failure if the whole thing is not immediately actualized. Thus if a poor man has a desire to marry into the aristocracy, and he does magick to this end, he should consider it a favorable result if he gets a job, say, as messenger for a brokerage house. It's not an introduction to the Countess Boeuf-Marrow's daughter, but it's obviously a step closer to his goal, and so he should not see it as any sort of failure. And it might be a quicker way to reach a state of wedded prosperity than by conjuring to promote some consciously contrived strategy, for instance to obtain a loan so he might attend florist school.

But with the astral none of these considerations apply. The target isn't some putative countess with a will of her own, but the elements of your own personality. There is no way the link could be any tighter, and if you've taken the trouble to develop your will with yoga and the disciplines of *Liber III*, there should be no question of who is stronger. Of course in some cases there might be doubt concerning the effectiveness of the means you have chosen—for instance my failure to manipulate my dreams by shutting down a single reflex. But for the basic work of silencing demons and transforming irritations into positive powers, the situation should be one of straightforward action and reaction. If things don't happen right away, you aren't doing it correctly.

This question of astral authenticity turns trickier when we address the astral representations of things outside our personalities—objects, people, events past and future, and so on. Is the source of the astral impressions "subjective" or "objective"? That is, does our astral impression of an external thing have its source in our unconscious perception of that thing—memories acquired during quite mundane contacts—or does each thing have an astral identity of its own, one we are able to see with clairvoyant vision during our projections?

To begin, let me say that even if the truth lies in the first alternative—that our examination of things on the astral simply makes conscious what we've already perceived unconsciously—that does not discount its value. Our subliminal perceptions of things surely do absorb facts about those things that our conscious minds ignore, gloss over, or dismiss. For instance, our conscious impressions of a person may be colored by what we need, want or fear from that person. We might have a favorable opinion of a promoter because we would profit financially if the deal he proposes were to be consummated, even as our more accurate and yet subliminal impression is that he is a thief. This impression could be unearthed through astral projection.

The alternate view here is that the essence of all things is contained in the Akashic Record or Astral Light, and that when we project we access this record.

The problem with the first option is that there have lived spectacularly gifted clairvoyants who have hit quite distant nails on their heads enough times to defy all talk of subliminal insight. Swedenborg, Rasputin, and Edgar Cayce come immediately to mind, and it's the sort of thing that authors like Colin Wilson like to write about a lot. The problem with the second alternative is that even these very gifted individuals were far from being right all the time. In fact, they verged at times on the outlandish, implying that the Akashic Record, if it exists as an objective thing, absorbs fantasy as easily as fact. Cayce's assertion of a mid-Atlantic Atlantis, for instance, has been thoroughly contradicted by undersea mapping by nuclear submarines, this showing that there is simply nothing down there but the mid-Atlantic rift. Yet according to Colin Wilson writing in his *Occult*, Cayce could read people's illnesses and prescribe treatments from great distances; "the patient did not have to be present so long as Cayce knew *where* to find him," the conclusion being that he could "leave his body when under hypnosis, and examine people in other places." (p. 167) He wasn't just probing unconscious minds that were right in front of him; there had to be either a "sea of mind" for him to swim through that was analogous to space, or some psychic part of him had to separate from the physical part to travel through physical space to meet and examine his patients.

Interestingly enough, both these alternatives support another great occult supposition—that there exist discarnate intelligences, beings that reason, perceive and act without the foundation of a physical corpus. If there exists a "sea of mind" like the Akashic Record, there is every possibility that it supports and is inhabited by purely mental "fish," while if instead it is possible for minds to move through space without a body, there is every reason to believe there might be some for whom this is the normal situation.

This notion of discarnate intelligences is an old one in magick, and is the essential assumption behind Aleister Crowley's Cairo Revelation. As one who accepts *Liber AL vel Legis*, I thus find myself stuck with it, even though Crowley in his later life took the liberty of identifying Aiwass with his Holy Guardian Angel. For myself, I don't hear its voice in any of Crowley's later writings— certainly not in any of the so-called Holy Books—but be that as it may, Crowley always saw the HGA as an independent being any- way, and not any sort of Higher Self. If "Higher Self" is identified with ego feeling compassionate and full of reverence, a pastiche of everything a person thinks "good" about his or her personality, then I would readily agree with Crowley. In any case I'm not at all sure what Crowley would think of my "spiritual supervisor" model for the HGA, even though to my reading it's exactly what Abramelin and Abraham the Jew were working to call up.

But then perhaps Aiwass isn't the best example. The prophecies are a bit too general and the symbols they are couched in could easily have been worked out ahead of time in Crowley's unconscious. Although I accept the book, it's still too easy for a dedicated debunker to attack it. Better examples may be found in Crowley's dealings with some of the lesser spirits he encountered, including Amalantrah and Ab-ul-Diz, whose stories may be found in Chapters 70 and 85 of Crowley's *Confessions*. They are distinguished by significant prophecies and numerical coincidences from out of the mouths of Crowley's mistresses, coincidences that were actualized by events coming from places beyond Crowley's sphere of control. Thus unless we wish to dismiss him as a liar, we are pretty much stuck with the independent spirit hypothesis, though of course this still leaves wide open the question of just what these spirits really are. By their works we may know them, but though these works tell us something certainly is there, they don't say a whole lot about precisely what.

His results clearly demand further study.

First published in *Chaos International* nos. 13 and 14, London, 1992–1993.

# The Integration of Alienation Through Correct Barbarous Syntax

## I. The Enemy Within

This essay concerns ways to become a well-adjusted wizard rather than any sort of empowered fanatic.

It is an unpleasant fact of magickal life that competence in the practice of magick in no way guarantees its safety. Magick is a psychic technology, and progress in magick brings the magician ever greater access to the psychic energy that he or she can use to manufacture his or her world in accordance with his or her purposes. But just what is it that determines the magician's purpose? Is it a rational response to circumstances, some personal or cosmic necessity on the order of True Will, or does it come from one or another of the spirits that comprise the mundane personality of the magician? Although increased psychic energy provides greater power to manufacture circumstances, it also produces a stronger emotional response to events. In sorcerous terms, such a response will be executed by one or another of these spirits, so if we cannot manage them, they will be able to tap into our power whenever circumstances call them into consciousness. And the more power we have, the more exaggerated and unruly will be their response.

The problem of emotional intensification has in traditional religion been solved through a great renunciation. Buddha taught that all was sorrow and the root of sorrow was desire. Paul of

Tarsus said you have to reject the flesh in favor of a life devoted to the Risen Christ. And the Jews learned to move all human passion along the rails laid down by their law, and the seemingly endless texts that interpret it.

Clearly none of this is suitable for sorcerers, who must be able to love Nuit, who is all things, and must honor the world her sister. We must be able to act out our love for them without restriction, in accordance with will. We must never stifle passion or cut it down, but instead must develop techniques to cause it to serve will, in one way or another.

The passions to which a wizard can succumb are not different in type from those afflicting non-initiates, but vary only in their intensity and in the fact that they often take on an occult motif. In any case they have common roots in primate psychology, and so the great errors of wizards are not so very different from the seven deadly sins: avarice (Saturn), gluttony (Jupiter), anger (Mars), pride (the Sun), lust (Venus), envy (Mercury), and sloth (the Moon). Whichever the wizard tends toward, the wizard must learn to manage it as he or she gains the power that energizes passion as well as creativity and conjurations. Lack of control that in a normal person would give rise to nothing more than occasional embarrassment can lead an empowered wizard to great errors that cripple his or her career. The power can turn a minor distortion of personality into a creative force and make the wizard's life its apotheosis in the world.

Examples of such extreme failures range from the Emperor Julian to Charles Manson, but most remain unnoticed beyond a small circle of friends. Greatness requires duration, and indulgence in the fault makes that impossible. So the work of self-correction needs to be perfected by all practitioners. Even in the case of great mages, it is a work that is often not done well enough. Some examples:

Aleister Crowley made occasional reference to a feature of his personality that he called "the Demon Crowley," and admitted that significant aspects of his behavior were out of his control. Examples of extreme manifestations of his personal inadequacies are provided in Regardie's *Eye in the Triangle*, Victor Neuburg's diaries as excerpted in Fuller's *Magical Dilemma*, and many accounts of Crowley's life written since his death.

Austin Osman Spare on occasion let his feelings of persecution and cultural alienation get the better of wise career strategy. When he published *The Anathema of Zos*, he needlessly alienated the entire set of his potential patrons. He would later refer to this publication as "a rash act."

And Dion Fortune never seemed to be able to admit that an active sex life could reverberate through one's magickal and spiritual endeavors.

Of course in none of these cases were the faults entirely crippling. But then who can say what these mages might have accomplished had they been able to master them? Crowley needed worthy acolytes to help him establish his Word as Magus, but so often he would squander their financial contributions on jewelry, liquor and cigars, and return their loyalty with casual betrayal. Spare needed to at least stay on terms with that class of Englishman who patronized the publication of books and journals of fine art, but in *Anathema* he insults them in an extreme and gratuitous manner, far beyond what was required for him to maintain his integrity in his dealings with them. And Fortune's distrust of sexuality must have been especially inhibiting to her research into the dynamics of the subtle body, wherein sexual energies count for so much.

It is as if each mage's most effective opponent lives within his or her own psyche, and that however adverse circumstances might become, it will be the internal saboteur that does the most to prevent the mage from accomplishing his or her task. Admittedly these three magicians struggled against great opposition and endured unremitting frustration. But then so do we all to a greater or lesser extent. If we allow this frustration to empower demons whose principle effect is to make success impossible, the frustration will only be augmented, and hence the power of the demons also, creating a negative feedback loop that will overwhelm psyche.

Of course one barrier that keeps us from dealing with internal opposition is the notion that we already know everything we need to triumph over it, if only we can summon the strength of will and character necessary to apply this knowledge. Crowley and Fortune asserted that they possessed the True Keys to the Mysteries. Spare countered that the True Keys were within ourselves, and declared that he knew how to find them. Thus one should simply conjure the correct gods to compel the appropriate demons to conform to one's high purpose, or do the automatic drawing and design the necessary sigils. And if the demons grow no weaker, or subtly change form to carry on their work even as they retreat from the sorcerer's direct attack, that must be a reflection on the discipline, purity or moral worth of the sorcerer.

Now in this I must disagree. I think instead that such a failure demonstrates an inadequate technology for manipulating psyche, and if there are elements of a sorcerer's psyche that have "minds of their own," that just means that his or her work of sorcerous research and development has not yet been completed.

This notion of psychic components having "minds of their own" is a good place to start. If you have aspects of your personality that tend to work against your essential purpose, this is an indication that these aspects have somehow been separated from the rest of you. The reason they get loose is usually because we push them away or repress their normal expression. This alienation of a part of ourselves twists its action and ejects it to a realm beyond conscious control.

By recognizing self-alienation and repression as the origin of our troubles, we discover a tactical opening that is especially advantageous to us sorcerers. To a sorcerer, whatever might have been alienated should be available for an astral inspection, and thus opened to magickal controls. Then we need only puzzle out the right strategy for addressing it, and bring it to bay.

All sorcery aside, the critical role of alienation and repression has been recognized by each of the giants of psychotherapy. Freud started it all by seeing the repression of sexual energies as the root cause of neurotic behavior. Adler said the same about repression of the will to power. Freud's colleague Wilhelm Reich countered that it was indeed sexual repression that did it, so the solution was to work politically to encourage a relaxation of arbitrary social restrictions on sexuality. Freud countered that the status quo had precedence over individual happiness, and Reich was sent on his way. And Carl Jung summed it all up by stating that neuroses could come from repression of any primal drive, or the rejection of an archetype also.

Once Freud had discovered repression as a force that could shape psychic content, the notion was quickly assimilated by the magickal community. *Liber AL* led the way, shouting out, "It is a lie, this folly against self." In his *Liber Aleph*, Crowley repeatedly notes repression's role at the heart of mental sickness and the distortion of will. Referring to the repression of sexual desire, he wrote that either the force that imposes the repression is victorious, and spawns the mental pathologies, "or the Revolt against that Force, breaking forth with Violence, involves Excesses and Extravagances." (p.3) As for Dion Fortune, the protagonists of her novels generally suffer from some symptom of repression. Sometimes this repression is rooted in immediate inclination or circumstances; sometimes it owes its origin to actions committed in a prior incarnation. And Austin Spare raised repression to the level of technical respectability, for he made it the key to his method of conjuration.

In Spare's method repression is used as a means for splitting off the energy of one's purpose so it can work independently, without risk of untimely discharge through fantasy, fear of failure, or lust of result. The sorcerer gives the energy its direction by putting the purpose into sigil form; the sigil is energized with free belief, inarticulate enthusiasms, or blood or sexual secretions; and then all recollection of the sigil shape is intentionally suppressed—driven out of consciousness until it is time to repeat the operation or else it is successful. The repression here is a ruse. It is no sort of expulsion of emotion carried out against a part of self that one hates or fears, but instead is a conscious strategy applied to make actual what one most fervently wishes.

With Spare's innovation repression was elevated from its role as "a cause of mental disease" to a more objective "tool for manipulating mind." Repression is a sure and certain technique for generating alienation, for dividing mind so the parts work independently, whether for good or ill, reflexively or as part of an occult strategy. With this we can consider mental alienation as a thing in itself, a fact of nature without any necessary connection to weakness or pathology.

Alienation is a making separate. It is a splitting off of a part of one's mind so it acts according to its own agenda. But this can be no simple forgetting. If an urge, emotion, or other mental impetus has so little energy that it can simply slip out of mind, it has too little energy to act anyway, and so is essentially irrelevant. Repression productive of alienation must be an effort, a struggle—painful if pathological, but in any case *work.* Only then will it result in the true separation that creates an actor who is genuinely independent, whether it works as sickness or as sorcery.

Energy flow is also important to the lifespan of an alienated mental actor. If there isn't a steady supply, the actor will turn comatose and enter irrelevancy. But if an alienated actor receives a steady supply of power, it will continue to act. For the conjurer, this indicates a need to continually recharge sigils until a work has been firmly accomplished. For the one who is sick from alienation, it implies a strategy for healing—which is to say, identify the energy source in its most primal aspect, then redirect its power in a way that reintegrates it back into the psyche, thus leaving the pathological actor to wither as if cut off.

The wizard who is successful at such a redirection will also have the primal energy as a new assistant. For perhaps the first time in the magician's life, he or she may have all power working in his or her favor, instead of part of it working at cross purposes or even as an opponent. The great mages of the 20th century show us that this is a factor even in the careers of the most talented, and so certainly nothing any of us moderns may safely neglect.

The ways a twisted impetus might work against us depend largely on what kind of energy is being twisted. The Freudians say that all the many varieties of life-energy are variations on the sexual, but to me such a broad generalization just strips all meaning from the word "sexual." It seems more useful to find as many different types of power as we can, the better to draw practical distinctions.

By referring to the planets we get seven distinct varieties of power, one of which—Venus—is identified with the sexual drive. But there is also the Moon for imagination, Mercury for discrimination, the Sun for execution, Mars for aggression, Jupiter for organization, and Saturn for acquisition. Each power is essentially benevolent if given an outlet for its free flow, but if it is stifled there will be stagnations and floodings. Of course the seven planets are just a rough guide, and one may well want to make a more detailed map as one goes along. So to generalize I'll just say that any primal impetus will act out, and if this is in any way prevented, it will act out in a less than optimum manner, and it will pain us.

Whatever type of energy is repressed, either the repression works or it doesn't. If it works, the energy is stifled, festers, and attacks the physical or psychic corpus with sickness. If it doesn't, then the energy pushes through and the resulting "excesses and extravagances" overcompensate for what had been held back, producing a malignant version of the original impetus. So in either case there's a problem, either a passive sickness or an active sin, and this will be the aspect of the situation that screams most loudly for a remedy.

This most obvious source of trouble will be so conspicuous because it is also the most superficial. It is the external manifestation of the maladjustment, and thus the most available for readjustment through the sorcerer's art.

## II. The Sorcerous Solution

The crux of sorcery is that it deals with the occult forces as if they were individuals. Whether these forces be personal habits of thought or emotional response, elementals, traditional demons, or personifications of personal, cultural or archetypal energies, the sorcerer treats each one as a self-aware entity, a self-interested actor that the sorcerer may bind and compel to assist in the performance of his or her will.

As for what these entities might actually be, this question is given a thorough review in *Chaos International* no. 9, this in an essay called "Models of Magic" by the German adept Frater U.D. He proposed a number of different ways of looking at the question, boiling it down to "the spirit model," "the energy model," "the psychological model," and "the information model." In these respective schemes we may look at sorcerous actors as self-aware spirits, currents of energy, the consequences of psychological manipulation, or as packets of information. Frater U.D. adds that it is generally convenient to mix these models. We may take the spirit model as a working assumption, then operate the energy model to provide the impetus that will enable the spirits we manufacture to act to accomplish our wills. At the same time, we may find that certain psychological operations like intentional repression help us spawn spirits, and others like the use of the Neither-Neither principle generate free belief to energize them. Of course the way this energy is often focused is with an alphabetic sigil—a monogram concealing the essence of the wizard's desire—which is little more than a packet of information.

Now with all this I am in full agreement, but my first allegiance is to the spirit model, it being the most aggressive posture we can take to address whatever it is that we manipulate when we do magick. Even if an entity is only a spirit by convention—in its real behavior acting more like a psychic switch or servomotor, subroutine or pump—by treating it as if it were a self-aware entity, I can force a part of my unconscious mind into rapport with my will. Or I can force the psychic aspect of an elemental force into rapport with my will. Or I can force an atavistic current personified as a traditional demon into rapport with my will. The levels of working are vast and ontologically various, but the spirit model adapts to them all. Thus may I make all aspects of Mind subject to conscious considerations of strategy, until all available force has been brought to assist me in my magickal program.

To apply Frater U.D.'s models to our question of psychic integrity, we could say that the act of repression, best described by the psychological model, produces a backwards motion of energy alienated from conscious intention, forced into separation because according to our "ethical" ideologies and/or parental and social programming it should not exist at all. And yet it does, and so this energy turns in on itself, a self-empowered bit of information— which is to say, *action*—that we may address as a separate spirit and so attempt to control. We might say in summary that the spirit model is true because we can make it work. We have to have a psychic structure if we are to have an effective psychic technology. By using the techniques of astral projection, conjuring and so on, we can define psychic contents as spirits, and because they respond as spirits when we do so, they're real enough.

The relationship between sorcerer and spirit is personal, like that of liege lord to vassal, and you must always be stronger than any spirits you conjure and name. By thus distinguishing them, you make them into more potent actors than they would be in an unfocused state. Once so enhanced, they may be inspired to expand their roles at the expense of your well-being. Remember that even if they can display preternatural knowledge and power, that doesn't mean they are competent to run your life. You are the master, they are the servants, and never let them forget it.

So each *type* of action in, on, or by the psyche may be addressed as a separate spirit, including the pathological actors that we designate as demons. The worst of these will be the most obvious. As Crowley put it, demons are easy to call up "because they are always calling you." Once brought onto the astral vision, they may be bound to your will, but if only you are stronger than they. Such a binding will involve looking into the heart of the demon, recalling all the oppression and fear and small crimes that went into its special synthesis. When these can be faced down, the sorcerer can give the demon a name, usually a "barbarous" name, but in any case no sort of discursive description. Once named, the entity must be bound with a ritual charge. Henceforth its action as the producer of its special symptom may be switched on or off at will's command. No matter whether said symptom be a psychosomatic sickness or a mental loop or an outrageous behavior, the sorcerer need only call the demon's name and command it to be silent, and it will be.

All this would be clearer with an example. To this end I will offer the primal force of *aggression*: its behavior, the likelihood of its alienation, and a strategy for using sorcerous techniques to reintegrate it for service to the will. Readers can then adapt my strategies to their own aggressive spirits, or to spirits of any of the other six powers—or however else they wish to count them.

Now by aggression I merely mean expansion. *It is not necessarily offensive expansion.* It does not seek so much to pull entities or objects into its sphere, but to expand its sphere to encompass an ever-increasing domain of some sort or another. Thus all types of ambition participate in the aggressive form, since artistic, commercial or professional ambition is simply the recognition of a sphere one can encompass, and its subsequent occupation. Nor need the sphere have a prior occupant. Aggression at its best discovers value where none could see it before, makes it its own, and then distributes its bounty for its own profit and that of those who need it. In my own life aggression has had its most positive manifestation in my work to seek out and publish the mechanisms and techniques of practical magick. This is aggressive in that it is a penetration into a country that, in terms of modern culture, is entirely unexplored. It contains plenty of open space that one can take for one's own, a creative Land of Milk and Honey. But it is only available to those who dare master it. There are not so many of these that we need fear crowding anytime soon.

Ambition, expansion, and the creative urge to understand in order to control—all these are the benign aspects of the aggressive impulse. But there are others less positive, as we may note in the daily media display. Rage, abuse, violence, exploitation, belligerent fundamentalism and war all confirm humanity's servitude to Ire. Of course with much of this the burden of history complicates the psychology. Think how much easier life would be today if, say, the Christian Church had spent as much effort denouncing slavery as it did burning witches. Fat chance, and so the social alienation threatens even now to tear our nation apart. Thus does the revolt against repression "break forth with violence" in the political realm as well as that of psychology and interpersonal relationships.

But this essay isn't really about politics. Here we are looking at how aggression is repressed in the life of the individual, and how we can deal with the strictly personal alienation that results. One readily acceptable hypothesis is that repression of aggression begins in childhood, just as Freud suggested for sexual repression. The aggressive child is met with parental resistance. If there is no understanding, there is strife, and the child learns that might makes right. And even if parents and child reach an understanding, it is rare for such a youth to find it in the educational system. Rules there are made to be enforced, often in the stupidest possible way, and it is a refuge for cynics, professional bullies, timeservers, and clueless incompetents. And that's just the administration and faculty. On the student side, the aggressive youth must learn to deal with peer groups and cliques, consensus behavior and the unthinking conformity of all the children who have absorbed the notion that adult practice defines reality. All these work to stifle and twist expansive energies. With no experience in dealing with the power, the youth will almost certainly respond ineptly, rebuked for arrogance by the adults in his or her life, rejected as 'bad' by his or her peers. In time the situation might improve, but not by much. With the control gained with greater maturity, our subject may find the strength to completely stifle the expansive energies, or else restrain them even as they tug against the reins. In the first case they will turn against his or her person and sicken it. In the second there is the question of how well the restraint is managed. Will our subject have the strength to keep the energies confined in fantasy, or will they break out in his or her relations with other people, leading ultimately to detention and death? People who can keep them restrained may well end up leading "productive lives," even as their inner certainties proclaim the world an armed camp. But it's better than the alternative.

Thus it may remain for the average man, but for the initiate the situation will become too unstable to endure. His (or her) psyche will have been made coherent by his initiation, and he will energize it with the power he gathers through his disciplines and practices. So all aspects of his psyche will be strengthened, including any aspects of his aggression he had found it prudent to restrain. These will now be better able to push their way through into event, consequence, and all the trouble that entails. It then will be obvious to the initiate that he (or she) must take steps to manage them magickally, lest they lead to a speedy doom.

The best way to accomplish this is to deal first with the most irrational aspects of the problem. Only after these have been recognized as demonic and bound can the more subtle difficulties be understood, and strategies for managing them developed.

The habit of thought and response that is most ferociously unreasonable will be the unit of action most efficiently defined as demonic. The demon is the grossest, the stupidest aspect of the initiate's twisted energies; its habit of response is irrational, and only makes sense when it possesses the initiate, its voice defining a reality that makes strife inevitable. By objectifying the complex as a demon and then binding it, the sorcerer may turn it on and off as if it were a switch. The name controls the action and within the limits of its function, any named and bound spirit will act in response to its name. Thus may the sorcerer enforce mental peace, gaining a fresh motivation to hone his magickal skills.

And the sorcerer will need them. Binding a demon will remove a pathological outlet for the energy, but the energy itself will in no way be diminished. It will simply seek a less obnoxious outlet—which is to say, one more in tune with the reality of the situation. This does not mean it will be any less dangerous. Dealing aggressively with real opponents is more dangerous than jousting with delusionary foes, because the real ones hit back. But only by removing the delusion can the reality of our power flow be exposed. And then the sorcerer can actually start to manipulate it.

To be specific about all this, an initiate might be burdened with a voice in his head that tells him there are potential fights in every human interaction, a voice with the power to produce vivid fantasies of how these conflicts will blossom and how he will resist and attack and triumph! Of course none of these conflicts will have any basis in the reality of his circumstances, and so will never come to pass, so the voice's absurdity and thus its pathology will be obvious. The wizard will define it as a demon, work to conjure it up on the astral, and name and bind it. Thus will he gain the authority to silence it whenever it speaks, or else call it up if actual combat is forced upon him, since in a real fight, utterly vicious, uncompromising rage can be invaluable. Thus will our sorcerer skim the toxic foam of repressed aggression from the surface of his psychic vat and bottle it for use in special circumstances. But does the aggression now go away? Hardly likely. It is of him, and he is of it, and he must master its use if he is to find his glory.

So he will soon find the energy bubbling up again in a more appropriate form—perhaps through causing him to become more aware of, and more offended by, the genuine assholes he encounters in his daily life.

Here we come to a question of definition. Should the impetus behind such a habit of offense be personified as a spirit or as a demon? The demon our sorcerer had just bound would expect conflict from the most innocent encounters, and it would never be right. But assholes are ubiquitous, and they do tend to arouse resentment. So it's best to put aside the question of whether the habit of offense is malignant or benign, a demon or a spirit. What the sorcerer must do is simply decide it is a part of his psyche that he wants to bring under control, and then do it.

When I reached this stage in my own magickal career, I dealt with the spirit by calling it up for an astral inspection and binding. The inspection showed that "taking offense at assholes" is largely a reflexive reaction. An asshole might be defined as anyone who lets his aura flame out without regard for its effect on any of the other auras in the vicinity—perhaps by playing the radio really loud at three in the morning or weaving down the turnpike at 20 mph faster than the flow of traffic. Such psychic violence tends to deflate the auras of those it impacts upon, and taking offense is the way the victim provides the energy necessary for reinflation. But sorcerers have more efficient ways of accomplishing this than angry fantasy. Also, the more power the initiate accumulates, the more will the obsolete reflex of taking offense waste this power on alienation. Having named and bound this reflex, I am now able to shut it down so that a reverie that once could have lasted half an hour can be cut off in a few seconds.

I should note that this was slightly more sophisticated magick than meeting the foaming demon, and I did it with the assistance not of sigils and sacred letters, but of my Holy Guardian Angel.

The Holy Guardian Angel of sorcerous usage is no sort of winged heavenly chaperone, saving the sorcerer from himself, but rather the specific "metaspirit" first described by Abraham, son of Simon, in *The Book of the Sacred Magic of Abramelin the Mage*. For Abraham the Angel was a gift from God, Who gives it with His Holy Magic to those who follow His Will and fear Him. The Angel gives advice concerning the performance of the magick and assists the magician in managing the spirits who actually operate it. Although I've dropped most of Abraham's practice as archaic, I've found it convenient to keep this supervisory function for the Angel, treating it as a sort of foreman or personnel director who has knowledge of and control over all the spirits within my psychic universe. If I can imagine a quality of mind, or even define an elemental in the objective universe, my Angel will give me its name and the ability to control it to the extent of my possible rapport with it. With the spirits that make up personality, this control should be total, and a wizard well-acquainted with his or her Angel will find his or her biggest obstacle to manipulating psyche is not an inability to call up and bind any specific spirit or demon, but simply knowing which one to call up, and why.

I would stress that this formulation of the Holy Guardian Angel allows for no transcendental function. I would never ask my Angel to herself provide inspiration or visions of splendor, though I would expect her to call up and help me manage other spirits who could. By thus confining my Angel to this management function, I make her much more useful than any generalized bringer of holiness, and I also guard against any other spirits co-opting her authority to advance their own agendas. If a female spirit claiming to be my Angel told me that I wouldn't be holy if I bought a better stereo, I would know it must be an impostor, for the statement would be wholly outside my Angel's competence.

So with my Angel's assistance I named and bound the spirit that causes me to be offended by assholes. By saving vital force otherwise spent on denouncing them, I gained both a modicum of power and also a certain degree of tolerance. This was especially apparent once I learned to silence the spirit when I was offended by myself after I personally behaved like an asshole. To not be obliged to denounce oneself is a great relief, though the process does release enormous amounts of free belief, which should be immediately focused into a sigil, or otherwise used for magick.

With his level of power increasing and his Angel ready to assist, the aggressive sorcerer will be better able to face his genuine obstacle—the inertia of whatever plane it is his True Will to encompass. And yet as he addresses this inertia, his rage may return. Of course at this higher level his anger's speech will be more refined, the voice perhaps demanding an attack on what is truly corrupt. Should the sorcerer heed it then, and act? Never! True will acts in Silence, without lust of result, and in such a voice lust of result is conspicuous. And yet the tirades will be justified, and so may not be dismissed as demonic or as a foredoomed fight against human nature. So what should the sorcerer do about them?

In my own case the problem was brought to a head by my anger at the civil state. It is clearly something that deserves it, so obsolete and incompetent it has become. Not only does it intrude on realms of psyche that are none of its affair, but it is patently corrupt. Justice is available only to those who can afford it; we have the best legislature money can buy; the rich get richer; the poor get poorer; and the primary loyalty of the police is to the police, no matter how bigoted or depraved they might be. Constant instances of these facts occur at all levels of government and are duly reported by an equally corrupt media establishment. And yet it is surely a waste of energy to give in and act, driven by the outrage thus inspired. At best, it gets you into a lot of legal trouble. At worst it gets you killed. And yet I found I could not simply define the anger as a spirit and command its silence, for the word my Angel gave me to do this was worthless. My resentment was too justified to accept a mere dismissal, the anger too complex to be so easily categorized—the valid objection of a free soul to self-important power. It would not tolerate treatment as a mere reflex or habit of response. And so I knew I had to try a different approach.

What I decided to do was transmute it. At my behest my Angel generated a synthetic spirit whose function it is to transmute anger at the civil state into literary creativity. My Angel manufactured a brand-new spirit, and whenever I am angry at the state, it causes the rage to vanish if I have but the presence of mind to speak its name. Assuming that this vanished force is in fact going into literary creativity, the spirit is acting to redirect the energy behind my justified resentment so it acts in a way that assists my will instead of complicating it. And yet the new application is appropriate to the energy, since the empowerment of individuals is a consistent theme of my writing. So a wasteful distraction is transformed into a creative boost. As a friend of mine remarked after I told him of this magickal innovation: "Some writers need a cottage in the Hamptons to get going. You just need to read the morning paper."

This strategy works against any compulsive mental routine. Separate spirits can be synthesized to render out the power that animates legitimate fears of unavoidable situations, resentment from broken friendship, and the urge to pursue passing interpersonal conflict. Spirits can also be synthesized to exploit neutral but wasted emotions like anticipation, impatience, and lust of result. The energy thus extracted can then be used for anything from magickal power to good luck in love. Just make the spirit so it turns the energy behind a specific unwanted passion into a specific talent or power—one that is enough in synch with your will that the energy works in silence. A norm of Silence should be the goal because True Will needs no speech, being from above the Abyss and hence beyond the chattering voices of Choronzon.

But in spite of this new understanding, I hadn't made it yet.

## III. Correct Barbarous Syntax

In Part II of this essay I described a progressive approach to dealing with the unruly spirits in the initiate's psyche—chaining the most obviously pathological first so the more justified may be tamed and turned to good account. My particular innovation has been the manufacture of synthetic spirits whose sole purpose is the transformation of healthy and yet wasted passions into powers that can push my will, for instance anger at the civil state into literary creativity. But as I noted at the close of Part II, my approach did not work as perfectly as it should have, for the goal of mental Silence was not attained even after the technique of spiritual transformation had been perfected. Not that the problem seemed especially esoteric. The mental speech that resisted my efforts had a theme consistent with my aggressive nature: the defeat of legitimate opponents, real and potential, at some future time when I would have the power to be completely victorious. I seemed to be powerless to affect these fantasies. When I tried to silence them by calling on spirits synthesized to transform the energy at the root of them, I got no results at all. The fantasy continued until its energy exhausted itself, limiting my experience to its poor rut and wasting my power on defining situations that would probably never come to pass.

Then one day, possibly with the thought of this utter non-probability in mind, I changed tactics. Instead of treating these anticipations of ultimate triumph as instances of conflict or rage against the state, I treated them as *anticipations*. I called on my synthetic spirit that transforms the energy of anticipation into magickal power. And the fantasy went away.

It was as if I had been yelling at Fred to do John's job, so it wasn't getting done, and as soon as I caught my mistake everyone got to work and the problem was solved. The embarrassing part is that it took me two years to see what I had to do. But then in fairness to myself, I had to clear away the gross before I could see the fine detail. And anyway, it's better to be deliberate than aggressive when you're manipulating your psyche. Tortoise is better than hare. If you rush, you can break things. And it's hard to get parts. But leaving aside the question of timing, I should explain just what I did. As I noted in Part II, I did have a synthetic spirit designed to transform anticipation—specifically into magickal power. My idea was that I'd do better to use my energy to empower my purpose than to dream about what it would be like when I eventually accomplished it. The types of anticipation I had in mind when I asked my Angel to synthesize this spirit were on the whole positive—what it would be like when I got some money, what wonderful mail would be in my P.O. Box—and I had never considered applying it to anticipations of glorious victory over the corrupt minions of the power elite. Instead I had treated the angry anticipation as if it were equivalent to the energy that empowers struggle. This was an error, and so I found myself disappointed when the spirits I called to transform it were ineffective.

The *energy of conflict* and the *energy of anticipation of conflict* are of two types and wholly different. It is unreasonable to expect that a spirit designed to deal with one would have any effect on the other. Each is a unique powerflow, and requires a unique tool to manipulate it.

The energy of conflict provides a readiness to close with a real enemy in real time on a real plane—physical, economic, verbal, legal, sexual, social, political or textual—a collision which will produce real consequences and, to a greater or lesser extent, real destruction. The energy is connected to voluntary muscles, the sympathetic nervous system, and the endocrine system. It is immediate, and if it is inappropriate it must be dealt with immediately if disaster is to be averted.

Anticipation of conflict, on the other hand, belongs more in the realm of fantasy than emotion. The energy merely serves to run a series of mental expectations—visualizations, verbalizations, rehearsals of tone and posture and action. It can be carried out while staring at a magazine in a waiting room, and it may involve victory over an opponent you will never actually meet.

So obviously the two emotions, though superficially similar in a conventional sense, have different dynamics and must be distinguished if malfunction is to be avoided. Conflict is immediate. Anticipation of conflict is an idealization contingent on a future that does not yet exist. The energy of conflict demands action *now*, before the moment of opportunity passes, and so it is immediately dangerous. Anticipation of conflict requires the manufacture of an imaginary reality that must have consistent duration if we are to find comfortable homes within it. It might ultimately be a crippling bother and a waste, but it won't start a fight *now*. The energy of real-time conflict, on the other hand, pulls us forward into action, and these days as small an act as making a rude gesture in traffic can get you shot.

By treating my anticipation of conflict as if it were real conflict, I was treating it as if it were more dangerous than it was, even as I was making it less respectable than the "benign" anticipations I was even then rendering into magickal power. To all these benign anticipations I applied the same synthetic spirit—call it "Donnersolz"—as if there were no difference between anticipation of a hot date and anticipation of good mail. In fact, I was even using Donnersolz to defuse anticipations of upcoming events that could be seen as unpleasant, for instance a trip to the dentist. To treat all these anticipations as equivalent, even as I relegated anticipation of conflict to that most dangerous class of conflict itself, was to subtly disrespect it, and to disrespect a tendency of psyche is to make it alien. Of course all anticipations may be seen as distractions and wastes of energy, but it is vital that we not play favorites. Such habits are of us, and to say that most of them are benign but *this* one is *nasty* is to send the nasty one to a place where we can no longer control it. We can say that they are all inefficient, and for that reason choose to reroute their power into more productive endeavors. But we must treat them all as equals as they arise in mind. At present, besides using Donnersolz to render the power from anticipations of conflict and victory over the civil state, I have even directed it to transform anticipations of my own death, and it has gathered the power for me.

And so we come to the source of the title for this essay, since the names of all the spirits are as a class known as "the barbarous names of evocation." Since they serve as labels that distinguish the elements of the sorcerer's psychic swarm, they may be said to serve as a language of psyche and power. But it is a speech that has direct and immediate effect. It is a language of conjuration rather than communication. It is concerned with powerflow, the *action* in any given circumstance, not the *objects* that make up that circumstance. (Living tissue is no object, but an activity.) Action is immediate; objects are simply what is left over from past actions. Reality is the objective residue of a subjective process. *What comes next* is an ongoing collective effort. Individual contributions vary.

The language that describes the residue of objects and their interrelations is that of discursive speech. The language of powerflow is that of the barbarous names of evocation. It is the difference between language that describes a reality and language that *in itself* manipulates reality through its intrinsic rapport with Psyche, which permeates all things inner and outer on all planes.

The elements of barbarous speech are the elements of the unconscious mind—on any level from your personal unconscious to the Mind of God. To speak the names is to activate them, and if they be properly bound, you may manage them to the extent of your rapport with them. Thus spirits that are part of your personal unconscious should ideally be available for total control, while the only control you can reasonably expect over an elemental is the ability to keep body and soul together while you take whatever bit of its power that you are able to snatch.

In appearance and pronunciation, the elements of barbarous speech will seem to be nonsense words—words like "Bartzabel," "Brazelsnatz," or "Babalon-bal-bin-abaft"—the specific vocabulary determined by the sorcerer who uses them. In Qabalistic magick, barbarous names were often created by stringing together symbolically appropriate Hebrew letters. For myself, I generally go more for the inspiration of the moment. Of course any wizard's barbarous names will have meanings that may be translated into discursive terms—for instance "the name of the spirit that transforms anger at the civil state into literary creativity"—but it is important not to let these into one's barbarous speech, since discursive thinking breaks the rapport between intent and the deep psyche that is required for effective magick.

At this point it might be helpful if I provided a selection of the parts of barbarous speech. To this end I offer a loose quotation from my *Stealing the Fire from Heaven*, where I presented the following categories of "sacred letters," which is to say, spirits.

1) Locations and structures in the psyche. These can include everything from abstract generalities like "the ego" and "the unconscious" to specific elements like chakras, Kundalini, and the power flows that connect them, and also elements of the astral landscape that you discover during your explorations there.

2) Ways or powers to take you from one location in your unconscious to another. These are especially important for astral projection.

3) Powers to manipulate locations and structures within your psyche.

4) Conditioned reflexes, acquired as a response to your environment. These include things like driving a car, eating with a knife and fork, and looking both ways when you cross the street. Reflexes are there for a reason and are very dangerous to disturb, unless of course the environment that conditioned the reflex is no longer relevant, for instance prison or the jungles of Vietnam.

5) Forces you discover as being available to do your will. These could be anything from sexual attractiveness to a droll wit, from the ability to draw schematics in your imagination to the ability to detect insincerity in business transactions. Any power you can specify, you can conjure, and so will it require a barbarous name.

6) Demons: reflexes that generate uncontrollable moods, fantasies and actions. Demons are often acquired as a response to a twisted environment that had to be endured during the weakness and dependence of childhood. The adult, empowered wizard will

realize they are inappropriate to his current situation, and will make every effort to manage them so they no longer bother him.

7) Independent beings, whether met on the astral or out in the world. They may be elementals; representatives of other people or specific plants or animals; or discarnate intelligences.

8) Connecting links to other, 'external' entities.

9) Your Holy Guardian Angel.

And to this list from 1984 I would add a tenth entry:

10) Synthetic spirits created for the purpose of transforming counterproductive energies into those that will promote your will—for instance anger at the civil state into literary creativity.

Thus we see that the process of binding demons and creating synthetic spirits that I described in Part II uses only two out of these ten "parts of barbarous speech," and it will take up a similarly small percentage of the potential words in our barbarous vocabularies. The corrective words remove the inefficiencies from our psychic energy flows, but as we apply them we open up endless opportunities for a progressive empowerment, each aspect of which will require its own barbarous term.

The fact I must emphasize is that when you speak a barbarous word, you are engaging a unit of action. It isn't communication of an aspect of *being*, but the activation of a specific sort of *doing*. Thus in using it you must conform to the barbarous dynamic rather than any "rational" considerations of morality, social consensus, or ethical cause and effect—perhaps those same considerations that caused you to alienate the primal energy in the first place, way back at the beginning of your troubles.

In summary, then, I would assert that our abilities to perceive and act in correct barbarous terms are accurate measures of our sorcerous integrity—"integrated" in the sense of existing as a coherent whole, the opposite of "alienated." In this sense, progressively greater attainment in sorcery consists of a progressive fine tuning of the sorcerer's barbarous vocabulary and usage.

The psyche is an energetic phenomenon. Energy, in the form of attention, emotion and physical vitality, comes out. It must then be disposed of by consciousness. Consider that all sorcery is concerned with this flow of power. With the techniques of sorcery and our barbarous grammars, we can define channels for this force and then enhance, manage, and transform the energy that flows through them. We can split the power off through conjuring so it acts independently, read its currents through divination and spontaneous omens, tap it in its elemental form in nature, or store it through sexual disciplines and variations on Taoist yoga. We can even steal it from our fellows through some form of the vampyric act, though of course we will then steal the momentum of their power along with its intensity, and so corrupt our own. But if we are to avoid hurting ourselves, we must apply this technology with the same deliberation that we would use to apply a physical technology. Thus to close I will offer a comparison between the criteria for "truth" in the discursive realm of logical objects, and the barbarous realm of psyche and spirit.

Discursive truth requires an agreement among those who participate in it. Barbarous truth requires effective action on psyche.

Discursive truth must be internally consistent. Barbarous truth must be dynamically unbiased by any discursive considerations.

Discursive truth has predictive power. Barbarous truth must be reliable over time.

Discursive truth organizes an alien world that is indifferent to our descriptions of it. Barbarous truth keys an internal, psychic world. This world is very sensitive to nuance, so when we address it we must be careful not to stretch it out of shape. If we do, we distort our selves also.

Finally, discursive truth is a tool for designing contrivance—anything from a steel machine to a human institution—and once designed and fabricated it may be driven by any conscious impetus, from individual will to consensus to mere rote habit. Barbarous truth is a tool for imposing impetus directly, without contrivance. The contrivance comes in when you split the impetus off by conjuring for a specific result. But even as the energy thus enters the "objective" world, the barbarous relationship with the sorcerer is still subjective, the names a code for the conjurer alone. Any person who encounters the energy may code it in his or her own way, if it gets coded at all, perhaps according to his or her own barbarous vocabulary. Which is to say, there need be no barbarous agreement among the participants in a sorcerous interaction for that interaction to be effective.

First published in *Widdershins* nos. 1, 2 & 3, Santa Cruz, 1996.

# Making Worlds

The point is that it's better to make your own experience than to let your experience make you.

This essay concerns strategy, not sorcerous technique or any sort of investigation into what mechanism really and truly makes magick work. It does work, somehow, in one way or another, and with effort anyone with an open mind can make it work. But what happens after that? After all, a hammer works, too. You can use it to crack nuts, discipline your cat, or chastise your neighbor for his lack of attention to his lawn. But are these its best uses? Or in spite of its apparent purpose as an unbreakable breaker, does it perhaps have a more creative function?

These same considerations apply to magick. In popular lore, magick is conspicuously suited to getting money, sex and vengeance. And in this same popular lore, the sorcerer always ends up being hoisted on his or her own petard, the magick backfiring into the sorcerer's face and causing his or her own destruction. Nor is this popular perspective contradicted by informed practice. To simply conjure in a bald-faced attempt to get money is to solicit either a personal injury or a death in the family, the conjuration working to reify your value as an insurance beneficiary. To conjure Jane Smith into your bed is to risk getting Jane Smith, kicking and screaming, into your life forever. And to call up 10,000 devils and set them onto your boss is to create a universe where 10,000 devils live, and they all have your address.

But then as strategy this direct approach is about as subtle as using a hammer to set off gunpowder. In the case of money magick, there are more devious ways of getting something for nothing than just conjuring for it. Most obvious are those that involve gaming establishments. They are designed so that some of their customers will win money, and the means the establishments use to ensure that less is won than lost are vulnerable to psychokinetic influence. What is more obviously magickal than causing a ball to fall into the proper slot?

The problem is that this sort of work is about the hardest thing a magician can do. Magick is the manipulation of psychic energy, and since a roulette ball has no psychic component, making it fall "properly" would require the most brutishly poltergeistic sort of psychokinesis. So a more roundabout attack is required.

One that comes to mind is the possibility of evoking the elemental of a racetrack and sacrificing to induce it to empower your chosen horse. If you picked horses that could run and bet on them to place or show, this kind of magick could be a tidy little earner. So what's the downside here?

To find it we should look at where the money we intend to win comes from. Horse betting is parimutuel; the money is won from the community of bettors instead of from a bookmaker or the owner of the track. So in essence you would be using the elemental as a pump to create an imbalance of value—a higher "pressure" on your side, a relative "vacuum" on the side of everyone else. But in the absence of a perfect seal, it doesn't seem as if such a circumstance could last indefinitely. *Something* would happen. On an unconscious level you would be stealing from your fellow bettors, and on the unconscious all trails lead home. But since there are no unconscious police, you would have to expect retribution in the form of theft. This you could guard against by becoming proficient in the martial arts, and through taking extraordinary precautions to keep your possessions secure. But then there could be a risk of the discrepancy discharging as if it were an omen, resulting in an injury to yourself or your chosen steed. Or the elemental could plead weakness to justify ever greater demands for sacrifice, the fulfillment of which would lead to the criminal act that would be your undoing.

The avenues the "pressurized" value might take to relieve the "vacuum" are thus so numerous that it would be impossible to keep them all sealed. No one has the power to fight off the universe forever.

This dynamic is typical of any attempt to manipulate "what exists" to serve one's purpose, using magick to divert it from its normal course. The diversion may succeed for awhile, but there will be a springback—Fate snatching with its left hand what was taken from its right. This is similar to what happens when one uses a hammer to gain the upper hand in a lawncare dispute. There is a moment's satisfaction in "making things right," and then come the police, the handcuffs, the bailbondsman, the legal bills, and even a period of incarceration. In short, a hammer is not the right tool for that job. Rather, it is intended to put nails through wood, in this way attaching one piece of wood to another. So it's for making things.

Here we have the crux of this essay and the key to strategy in magick. The alternatives are clear. We can assume that we are stuck with what is already out there and use magick to try to manipulate it to our advantage, or we can use magick to try to make an advantageous world from scratch. Instead of just conjuring to get money, we can empower spirits that will help us manufacture careers that will enable us to generate value for ourselves and others. Instead of just conjuring to force Jane Smith into our beds, we can attract from the general population sexual partners who will be suited to our personalities and life situations. Instead of cursing our bosses with 10,000 devils, we can practice the technique of disconnecting from our auras the hostility that their abuse of authority generates, causing it to return to its point of origin and leave us to enjoy our worlds in peace. In all these cases we work as gods to create our own universes, according to our wills, rather than fiddling with the details of the creation of Somebody Else in a pathetic attempt to gain some little edge.

Of course this fabrication of perfect worlds does require power, but this is of little moment when we consider how much power we waste in any given hour defining worlds we'd rather not inhabit anyway. It's simple enough to use magick to smelt the power out of these imperfect worlds and use it to manufacture the realities we prefer. Our universes consist of our experience. Our experience is what we are aware of. Awareness *as such* is psychic energy, which can be directed as magickal power, and any awareness we have that is counterproductive or wasted may be converted to promote this manufacture. None of this has anything to do with fantasy wish-fulfillment. An event conjures unpleasant feelings or distressed memories or otherwise excites us to no purpose, so we use magick to extract the energy from our reaction and program this energy to promote some circumstance we need to actualize our wills. This will be a real circumstance and its successful manifestation will be recognized as reality by any and all outside witnesses. As such *it will take time*, but as Eliphas Levi reminds us, eternity is at our disposal.

My favorite technique for working such a conversion is the astral synthesis of specific spirits whose sole function is to transform specific counterproductive emotions into specific positive powers—for instance anger at the civil state into literary creativity. This technique will work for any unwanted emotion—despair, impatience, worry over job hassles, resentment, disappointment—and even those that are pleasant enough but are still a waste of energy, for instance fantasies of ultimate success. Of course one must also have the presence of mind to actually call for the aid of the proper spirit whenever one is possessed by such an emotion, but that is a matter of personal power rather than strategy.

Another source of energy is sexual activity, no surprise since fabricating new worlds is what sex is all about. Naturally it must never be stifled; if the occasion warrants and the magician has no partner, his or her hand will do quite nicely. But it must never be wasted. It has the power to create the universe you desire, if only you have the magickal technique to direct it toward that purpose. Not that this technique needs to be especially elaborate. Banishing, centering and so on are of course necessary, but once that's done, merely concentrating on a pertinent sigil during orgasm and then using the elixir as a eucharist or to charge a talisman is all that's required. The critical point is the discipline. Once one starts using sexual energy in this way, one crosses a threshold, and one cannot go back to using it for mere pleasure or the release of tension. It is as if the practice of sex magick gives one's sexual fluids a power they previously lacked, and if one then discards them promiscuously (wadded up tissues in the wastebasket, unbanished wet spots on the sheets), the energy in them will empower one's dominant demons, generating all sorts of trouble.

So much for emotion and sex. Other mental contents that might be exploited for magick include ideology, whose power may be rendered out through Spare's Neither-Neither; sentimental attachments, again with the Neither-Neither; elementals; and finally aesthetic rapture or any other unutterable ecstasies you have the power to bring to bay. Aesthetic rapture is available anytime a work of art (anything from music to architecture) moves you to such an extent that you physically feel the energy. This indicates that your subtle body has been excited, and so you may wheel the energy into your belly chakra for storage.

Other unutterable ecstasies include the adulation of a crowd, the intoxication of strange drugs, the satisfaction of career accomplishment or victory in a competition, and even physical terror. A good example of the magickal use of terror was given by Ramsey Dukes in his introduction to Austin Spare's *The Witches' Sabbath*, where he remarks upon his use of a carnival ride to inspire such terror to charge a sigil, even as he avoided any actual physical danger. Thus may food energy be converted directly to magickal energy.

To sum up, there is no aspect of excited consciousness that may not be exploited to assist in the manufacture of one's chosen world. It is only a matter of discipline. One must recognize power when it comes and not fall into habitual patterns of dealing with it, whether these patterns apply the power to the assertion of anger, despair, anxiety, or any other view of the world, whether political, sentimental, nostalgic, philosophic, religious, or even technologic. Even pleasure can be channeled to assist in the work of creation, though we should always remember that all work and no play make Jack and Jill dull children.

This last caution does not apply to sexual pleasure, since it's better when it's magickal anyway.

First published in *Chaos International* no. 18, London, 1995.

# The Subtle Body

The subtle body is the anatomy of Spirit that meshes with the anatomy of Flesh to animate organic tissue with consciousness, will and life. Its various components cover all aspects of this animation, from a straightforward management of vital force to the subtleties of speech, self-protection and emotional involvement. Through mastery of the subtle body, the integrity of the flesh may be enhanced and maintained even as creativity is made as much a product of craft as any sort of talent or gift—the craft of the sorcerer.

The two major schools of subtle practice are those of the Tantric Hindus and Buddhists, and of the Chinese Taoists. In this essay I will be using the terminology of the Tantrics, because it is better known, even as I take the attitude of the Taoists, because it better conforms to the attitude of the Western magician. For the Tantrics the goal of work on the subtle body is Liberation from the round of birth, death and rebirth. For the Taoists the goal is Transformation—the enhancement and empowerment of that body so it may better manage life in this world and, perhaps, maintain its identity through the whorl of death and so carry its momentum over into the new body to come. The Tantric strives for mastery over the subtle body so he or she can literally suck it up out of manifestation. The Taoist strives for mastery so he or she will be a master of living through it, fulfilling the purpose Tao had when it manifested to begin with. As Austin Spare put it, calling Tao "Kia," "Self-love in complete perspective, serves its own invincible purpose of ecstasy. Supreme bliss simulating opposition is its balance." To develop the subtle body is to gain the power to play the opposition right along with Kia—recognizing even birth and death as aspects of the simulation—and so share its bliss.

Though the Tantrics and the Taoists describe a similar subtle anatomy, their programs for developing it differ according to their purposes. Wishing to 'Liberate' themselves by pulling themselves back up into their sources, the Tantrics give their tag ends a strong definition right from the start. Then as the Tantric pulls it in, he or she defines the psychic structures it passes through, each in turn. The Taoists, on the other hand, define all the structures together at the beginning and then gradually strengthen them, making for a much more gradual, and hence easier, development.

The anatomy of the subtle body consists of energy centers, called chakras by the Tantrics, and the currents of Light that connect them. The most prominent and powerful of these currents is the well-known Kundalini. The flow of power that runs up and down the spine, it is pictured as a serpent sleeping at its base, one which rises up the spine whenever it is aroused, either by circumstances or the manipulations of the subtle technician.

Our spines thus serve as the fleshy foundations for our central columns of chakras, Kundalini, and related energy flows. This central column may be seen as the nucleus for our swarms of spirits, a structure of psyche anchored in body that is intrinsically more stable than they, the source of strength for will as we endeavor to organize these swarms to impose our purposes upon the world.

As I said, the terms "Kundalini" and "chakra" are Tantric, but the Taoist conception of the subtle anatomy is very similar. And Rosicrucian magicians have their own conception of it, which they call the Middle Pillar. But though the overall views resemble one another, the details differ significantly, even in such basic matters as the number of chakras. The Rosicrucians see five, the Tantric Buddhists six, the Tantric Hindus seven, and the Taoists about fifteen, though these vary in significance. For myself, I've found a use for about ten, and the way I see the power moving through them is very much like the Taoists. My main conceptual influence here has been the books and lectures of Mantak Chia, though I can't say he was anything more than a source of ideas. Once I had the ideas, I checked them with my Holy Guardian Angel, and when I had problems she provided me with additional information. So my presentation here should be seen as original research guided by the Chinese tradition.

A word of warning though: it is said, and I think I agree, that the subtle body we conceive of and reinforce with meditation and magick is the subtle body we get, that except for basic structures like the third eye, belly chakra and Kundalini it is mutable, scarcely even defined in the average man or woman, and with work it develops according to the scheme we impose upon it. If this is the case, it is important that our conception be open enough to include every center or current we might need. And it is imperative that our practice not contravene the interaction between psyche and flesh that is necessary for physical health. This, as we shall see, is not an insignificant risk, and so there is a need for caution in practice. Again, I should stress that my own progress has been guided by my Holy Guardian Angel, who in fact instigated my research during an astral interview wherein I was asking after something quite different. The names for my chakras and details for how to use them have all come from my Angel, and I have no idea how I could have done this without her help. Much came from Chinese yoga, but only because it was compatible with what my Angel prescribed. If it had not been, I would not have used it.

The ten chakras I use are located at the base of the spine, in the genitals, in the belly, at the solar plexus, at the breastbone, in the throat, between the eyes, at the hairline on the forehead, at the base of the skull where it connects to the spine, and at the top of the head.

The base of the spine is the main energy source for the subtle body. This energy is symbolized by the Kundalini serpent, which uncoils and rises up the spine in moments of creativity and excitement. It rises in anyone who has any real life in them, whether they've had occult training or not. What the occult training does is enable one to awaken the Snake at will, and also to raise it higher and with greater brilliance than one could without it.

The genitals are the valves for sending Light out into the world as a distinct entity—either as spirit or as flesh, depending upon preparation.

The belly is the energy center for bodily processes, and it is the focus for physical health. According to Chia (and my own experience confirms this), it is the only place where Light may be safely stored. I find that if my aura is filled with Light after meditation or if I am holding a eucharist in my mouth, I can draw the energy into my belly chakra, which will glow ever brighter. Chia stresses that this must be done after meditation because if one habitually leaves energy in the other chakras, it eventually causes damage.

The solar plexus is the chakra for sending Light directly out into the world. It is often active during poltergeist displays, when it may be a center of intense pain.

The heart chakra behind the breastbone has to do with the exchange of emotional energy between individuals.

The throat is for speech, and once this chakra has been magickally defined, one's words of power tend to get some real punch.

The third eye is for seeing into the depths of things, seeing them in terms of the powers they are, without the veil of our descriptions of them.

The hairline chakra is something that I know only empirically, in that a friend told me of its existence and I've never found anything to read about it. I got the details on how to use it from my Angel and have since then found that it functions as a source of "free" energy from somewhere "outside." The energy comes in at the hairline and can then be sent out through the solar plexus, providing a current of Light to charge talismans, eucharists, or other external targets without depleting one's own energies.

The base of the skull is for protection—"eyes in the back of the head."

The top of the skull admits Light from the Highest.

Once chakras have been defined, it is necessary to be able to open and close them at will. My approach was to treat each of them like any other sorcerous entity, addressing them one at a time during a series of astral projections. I named each with a "barbarous" name and then bound it with a formal charge, all with the assistance of my Angel. With my control thus established, I am now able to manipulate them simply by addressing them by name, either calling a chakra to open it or speaking a general word of closure to shut it down. This is my procedure for nine of them, the exception being the belly chakra where energy is stored. Here it is not a question of "open" or "closed," but whether the chakra is gathering energy in or is distributing it to some part of the body—generally to heal a specific physical complaint.

When I have energy to store, whether from a eucharist held in my mouth or some body-wide excitement, I call the chakra's name and imagine the spokes of a double wheel moving in opposite directions pulling the Light into their hub in my belly. Once the Light in mouth or body and also in the spokes of the wheel has dimmed, and only the hub still glows, I simply swallow (in the case of a eucharist), banish, and go about my business, trying not to think about what I just did.

When I have a physical complaint, I have a different word that causes the wheels to turn in their opposite directions, with the spokes delivering Light to the location of the ailment. In my own practice my mind's eye usually sees this location as black or red—that is, infected/necrotic or inflamed—and I use the Light to turn it into a bright blue-white. Two precautions should be taken. First, before you begin you should define your aura as a definite shell, either by banishing or by speaking specific words of power, this to keep your Light from leaking out into space. Second, when you are done you should speak your word for gathering in to pull any excess back into your belly for storage.

It is best to use this technique immediately upon noticing a symptom, since long-term ailments take on lives of their own that are difficult to extinguish. For instance, I recall a time when I tripped on some branches and fell on the sidewalk, landing on one hand and one knee. My hand and wrist didn't hurt at all, but the knee was alarmingly painful. So I filled it with Light, and it gave me no more trouble. The next day my wrist hurt, though it wasn't severe so I let it go. But it was persistent, and turning bothersome, so at the end of a week I filled it with Light. It was too late to do much, though, and it took months before it was entirely pain-free.

In any event, the naming and binding of the chakric functions are what makes such manipulation possible. And besides the chakras, you may also address in this way any of the connecting flows and get good results. With practice you will be able to carry out the circulation of the energy by using your names as a mantra to manage the currents, vibrating these names with full force in cases where particular power is required.

With the subtle body thus specified, it is necessary to activate it through practice. The way to do this is through meditation. Whether in a formal asana or while walking, swimming or listening to a rock & roll band, the magician visualizes his or her subtle body as an anatomy of flowing Light synchronized with his or her breathing. This is the underlying activity whenever one manipulates the subtle body, and so it must be a familiar exercise, and no sort of effort.

The approach one takes to meditation depends on one's approach to the psychic anatomy—whether one sees it as a Tantric or a Taoist. As I remarked earlier, the Tantric approach gives the tag end of the subtle body a strong definition right from the start so the yogi can begin to pull it up to its source, then defines each chakra that it meets on the way. This tag end is the Kundalini. The Tantrics say it sleeps tightly coiled at the base of the spine, having accomplished its work of manifestation, and to dissolve manifestation (which is what is required for Liberation) one must bring it back up to its source in the top of the head. To awaken it and start it on its trip upwards requires an extreme manipulation of vital force through the control of breath, called pranayama, a procedure considered to be dangerous if practiced without the guidance of a fully-realized guru. The Chinese approach, called "circulation of the Light," is both gentler in practice and less extreme in purpose. Transformation rather than Liberation is its goal, and to attain it the sage undergoes an inner alchemy rather than a withdrawal, synthesizing a subtle body whose energies are in harmony with those of the Tao that is the source of it and all things.

In its original form circulation of the Light is a meditation wherein the sage uses deep, steady breathing to run power up from the base of the spine, over the top of the head, down the chest and under the spine and back up, generating energy as it goes. The objective here is the brewing of a mixture of sexual energy, vital force and aesthetic energy which the sage can, upon cultivating them into an equilibrium, match up with their cosmic equivalent—Tao—to form an immortal entity called "the Crystal Child." It is a very elaborate discipline, and to follow it requires a full assimilation of the Chinese systems of yoga and aesthetic culture. What I offer here is a much simplified version, inspired by the Chinese approach but with very much my own stamp. And I would suggest that any readers who choose to follow this practice use what I offer in much the same spirit—as a source of ideas rather than any sort of cut and dried technique. It's your own body you're working on and you must conform to its needs and listen to its special feedback if you're to have any sort of success, and no sort of disaster, as you pursue this practice.

To begin this circulation, it is necessary first to arouse Kundalini, which you may do with breath and muscular contraction. To do this, when you inhale tighten in quick succession the perineal muscles and then the muscles right behind the anus, and imagine a Light moving up your spine, as if the contractions were push/pulling it upwards. (This movement may be accentuated by bringing yourself to a state of sexual excitement, then pulling (in the same way) the engorgement upwards instead of releasing it in orgasm.) Then with the exhalation, relax the muscles and visualize the Light flowing down the front of the chest (as the Chinese have it) or back down the spine (as I have it), depending on which feels more correct (and what your Angel tells you).

Though this Light from the base of the spine will be the most intense, you may find you are able to bring a stream of Light in from the top of the head. In fact, activation of the lowest seems to stimulate the highest. Once they are both open, if you chant the names for their associated energy flows as mantras, you can run the Light from above and below in and out simultaneously, sucking them in with the inhalation, letting them run back out as you exhale, turning your whole aura into a blaze of Light.

Unfortunately, unless closely contained the power here does not stay with the wizard who generates it. Like a fountain in the wind, it sprays all over his or her environment. What happens to it depends on what's there. The power can be used up in displays of bizarre events, or it can attract entities—spirits or people—deficient in energy that latch onto you like thirsty mouths onto a bottle of beer.

The solution here lies in the containment. Instead of just running the Light up and down the column, use it to create a smaller egg around your head—one encompassing your chakras from your throat on up and enclosing your point of view. On the inhalation the energy from below comes up the spine, through the base of the skull, over the top of the head and down the front of the face to tuck under at the throat and merge with the upward flow to form the egg. The energy from above comes in at the top of the head and follows the same circuit. Thus two types of power merge to form a single ovoid of spinning Light whose motion tends to pull additional power out of the top and bottom chakras.

Then on the exhalation the flow is reversed. Or instead of just letting it run out, the energy can be used to intone the name of a spirit or demon, or any other word of power for magickal working. And one can always sweep the energy into the belly, using the spokes of the double wheel to pull it in for storage in that chakra.

One important detail is what happens at the sides of the spinning egg, just outside the ears. You may find the Light tightening into vortexes there, and you will have the choice of letting them drain outwards or inwards. Inwards is the way to do it, for then it will be drawn into the point of view behind your eyes. Outwards I've never tried. My Angel tells me it's a bad thing to do.

Now I must stress the necessity of always monitoring whatever feedback your body gives you as you carry out this circulation. For instance, in about my third year of practice, in the midst of great success at using the Light generated in magick, I began to feel strange sensations in my feet and lower legs, which I had not included in my circulations. They felt as if their blood flow were inadequate, or perhaps as if I had suffered some nerve damage. But a consultation with my Angel gave me the answer. In focusing all my attention on my upper body, and confining my visualizations to the Light that circulates there, I was depriving my legs of the power they needed. Naturally in the beginning of my practice this didn't matter, since my circulation was more imaginary than real, but as I gained competence my lack of attention to my legs really did leave them out of the flow and bring on physical symptoms. So I defined separate currents for them, and for my arms, also. For my legs I split the flow out of the basal chakra to send two dimmer, secondary streams down the front of my legs to my feet and then up the back of my legs on the inhalation, and reversing it when I exhale. For my arms I defined similar flows split off from my upper back. This solved the problem immediately. And fortunately I consulted my Angel before I mentioned my symptoms to a medical professional. If I'd told a doctor I probably would have been beggared by the tests and then put on some awful drug that would have destroyed my ability to read my subtle feedback, and all this without solving the problem. So if you're doing work like this and encounter any symptoms that might be related to it, always try first to solve the problem in terms of the work. Then if that doesn't help, by all means go ahead and see a doctor. But to expect a doctor to understand what work on the subtle body is all about is to expect the moon and the stars.

With this last correction I completed the basic definition of my subtle anatomy. But once defined, this new thing must be energized to give it sufficient force. Four approaches stand out here: magick, music, drugs and sex.

The principle magickal techniques that I used involve eucharists dedicated to each of the chakras, and astral manipulation. The most basic astral manipulation is simple penetration. To do this I would go onto the astral, define the chakra as an orifice, go through it, stay a few minutes, and then come back. I didn't usually learn all that much from the vision itself, but in the week or so following I found that events occurred that were related to that chakra, and in any case the procedure made the chakra more apparent and easier to use.

I followed this with a number of further manipulations, mostly involving a definition of my ten separate chakric flows at different levels of my astral structure. These procedures were too complex to be described here, nor should they be described. My astral structure is something that I alone need to know, and such practices are excellent ways for other people to search out theirs. They'll find it's easier if their Angels go along to help them, though.

Music, on the other hand, is not personal at all, but on the contrary is capable of causing a whole stadium full of people to enter a simultaneous rapport with a flow of power. The best example of this is the rock & roll concert, and rock music is notable for having a conspicuous effect on the subtle body.

A few years back I read a piece by a music reviewer who, in denigrating the Sixties, remarked that it was a time when people "thought they could find God in guitar solos." To which my immediate reaction was, "Well, can't you?" Which is to say, electric blues rock & roll arouses the Kundalini, and the rise of the Snake is a precondition for any manipulation of power. On the most physical level this arousal is accomplished by making you want to move your pelvis in a rhythmic, sinuous manner that is very arousing to Snakes. It is a motion that makes them want to *move*, and of course the only way they can go is *up*! On a more esoteric level, it is true enough that rock (and also jazz and other musics with African rhythmic roots) can arouse Kundalini even when one is sitting rigid in a chair. And this brings us to our third method of subtle enhancement—drugs.

The best drugs for this work are cannabis and the psychedelics—all illegal, of course. But this illegality does not stop them from making the subtle flows conspicuous to the meditator's inner eye. Also, proficiency in circulation of the Light makes it much easier to control the psychedelic experience. So it's a nice positive feedback loop that may be enjoyed with minimal toxicity—unless of course a specific drug is incompatible with your specific body chemistry. But, alas, still illegal.

After rock & roll and drugs, there can only be sex remaining, and so it is. The crux here is that orgasm is a discharge of vital force. The act splits off the Light, something that must not be done promiscuously, but only for a purpose that justifies the loss. Thus when one has an orgasm for less than cosmic purposes, it is essential that the energy be reabsorbed. This not only prevents its loss, but keeps it from being stolen by other entities to advance their own agendas. Such beings might be anything from other people to discarnate intelligences to personal demons alienated from one's own psyche. Once they find a food source, they'll generally exploit it until they exhaust it, to the obvious detriment of the careless yogi.

The traditional Tantric and Taoist solution to this problem is not abstinence, but retention of semen through inhibition or redirection of ejaculation. Chia stresses that orgasm is not discouraged in Taoist yoga, but on the contrary is made all the more intense when ejaculation is inhibited. And Tantric yogis are renowned for their ability to suck up fluid with their penises, including semen and vaginal secretions, thus keeping the prana from being wasted.

Now aside from inoculating the yogi's urinary tract with all sorts of bizarre pathogens, such disciplines are a lot of work, so in keeping with that venerable Western dogma, "Ease of Use," I offer the following alternative. To wit: *treat sexual secretions as eucharists.* Unless you wish to use them to charge a talisman to influence the "objective" world, place them in your mouth and hold them there while you wheel their Light into your belly chakra for storage. When the Light dims, swallow and banish. (It's a good idea to banish before you begin to "manufacture" them, too.) Some practicalities:

Men have it easier here than women, but that shouldn't discourage the ladies. For self-stimulation, men need only ejaculate into a container. But women will need something like a piece of bread to soak up vaginal secretions and so prevent their loss. Of course the woman can wheel in that Light that remains in her vagina as well as what she holds in her mouth.

For intercourse, the classic method is oral sex after ejaculation, with the man gathering the "elixir" from the "cup" in his mouth and sharing it with the woman. Any elixir that cannot be retrieved can be dedicated as a libation to Our Lady Nuit and, again, its Light may be absorbed by the woman as she wheels the Light in from the eucharist. For those who would rather not have mouth-genital contact (mouths are always septic; genitals should not be), the use of condoms and bread could serve. In fact, one could empty the condom into a glass of wine or fruit juice (low-alcohol is easiest on the little sperms), drink it with the bread, and be almost Romish about it.

For anal sex condoms are a must, as much because of the difficulty of getting at the elixir as the need to guard against disease.

To close I would reemphasize the discipline of chastity, the need to treat all sexual secretions as holy fluids brimming with power that must never be wasted or profaned. As you gain proficiency in these practices, your power will begin to become significant, and so must be kept under control if misfortune is to be avoided. Such misfortune will be a direct consequence of either subtle exhaustion or else independent entities using your power for their own purposes. The way to keep this from happening is to keep your power to yourself.

This leads to the subject of vampirism, wherein the vampire absorbs the victim's sexual energy without offering any of his or her own. Here I will simply say, *don't do it!* It is a self-destructive vice. The rush of energy one obtains upon feeding is extraordinarily pleasurable, and so the practice is extremely addictive. But the power carries with it the momentum of the victim, and so is the vampire's own momentum corrupted. The result is a sort of psychic bloat, followed by physical decrepitude. There is no profit in it.

This essay is an adaptation of an essay of the same title first published in *Chaos International* no. 9, London, 1990.

# Sending Power
# to Help and Hurt

*"I am not I; I am but an hollow tube to bring down fire from heaven"*
— *Aleister Crowley*

## I. The Dynamic

The giving of energy has a long tradition in healing, and is also intrinsic to the doing of magickal hurt. What is often not realized is that the same power can do both. In fact, to curse safely it should be the same. Sending evil after evil only augments the malignancy; sending beneficent energy makes for a much more *interesting* reaction.

First we will cover the psychic plumbing in general, then the specific valves that need to be opened, and then how it can all be used.

As one might expect, the plumbing involves the chakras and the energy flows between them. Of course what chakras there are and where they are in the aetheric anatomy is a matter of some dispute, and you really should do your own research, but you have to know the results of mine to understand this essay, and so I give it here. According to my results, there are ten. These are located at or around 1) the base of the spine, source of the Kundalini; 2) the genitals, center for reproduction, whether physical or aetheric; 3) the belly, center of physical health and the only place power can be safely stored; 4) the solar plexus, the opening for sending energy outside; 5) the heart or breastbone, the opening for emotional contact; 6) the throat, the center for Speech; 7) the third eye, for Vision; 8) the hairline, an orifice opening to a source of free power; 9) the base of the skull, for warning; and 10) the top of the head, the opening to the Infinite.

My first attempt to send energy occurred when a friend of mine was told she had an internal growth that should be removed. I felt that if magick was worth studying at all, it should be able to help here, so I visualized her receiving the same sort of Light I visualize for myself when I'm sick. This may or may not have helped, but it made me feel as empty as a week-old jack-o'-lantern, and about as moldy. Clearly the wise wizard did not heal others by killing himself, so there had to be another way to do it. I recalled that many healers just acted as conduits to send power brought in from somewhere else, and when I went onto the astral to ask my Angel about it, she confirmed it. Pull it in through the hairline chakra, she told me, and send it out through the solar plexus. She gave me a word with which to send it and a word to pull it back, and told me to shut my chakras and banish when I was finished. So that's what I did. The energy streamed out to envelop my visualization of the woman (who was, of course, miles away). When she seemed to be soaked in Light, I pulled the stream back, closed my chakras, and banished. I did this several times, the last the night before her surgery. It was a cyst full of fluid and now she's fine.

I must say that healing with this technique is problematical. It is quite likely that my friend was not all that ill. If the energy did anything, it simply hastened her surgical recovery. But the problem is more than one of verification of effect. Subsequent research has convinced me that for more complex ailments, this technique is about as appropriate as trying to rebuild a carburetor with a pair of pliers and a claw hammer. The procedure surely does energize, as we shall soon see, but if a person is suffering from any sort of maladjusted energy function—anything from an autoimmune disturbance to cancer—more energy just rammed in could make it worse. Of course there are energy healers who enter into a close rapport with their clients and so are capable of using their own energy to realign the misalignments. And it is possible, I suppose, to use the techniques of magick to better attain this rapport and effect this readjustment. May be. But who wants to enter rapport with a bunch of sick people? When you consistently work to attain psychic intimacy with disease, it's difficult not to pick it up yourself, no matter how well you purge yourself after each session. Energy healers are not known for being the healthiest people in the world.

But then as stimulation to the healthy, this technique can be very interesting in its application. To offer a most basic example: one evening my cat brought a flying squirrel into the house—very much alive and uninjured—and it escaped with such speed and agility that we could not follow it to the place it hid. The cat, best equipped with ears and nose to find it, hunted with us for awhile but then tired and lost interest. So I sent her some energy. She immediately resumed the search and soon was pawing a likely hiding place. The cabinet was moved, the squirrel was netted, and both it and the cat went outside to settle their differences. But the reaction you can get from people is better still.

The one big thing I couldn't do with this power was give it to myself. I thought of trying, but when I asked my Angel she explained why it would be a bad idea. When I sent power out through physical space to impact on another person (or the cat), any excess dissipated in space and did no harm. But if I were to send it to one of my own chakric spaces, any excess would be trapped and could do some real damage. We're tubes, and to cap one end can bring on a bursting.

There was, however, another way to benefit personally. I found that if I sent it to bands doing rock & roll shows, it seemed as if they played better. Instead of just doing songs, they would get into long, complex jams, sending me into far space indeed! Since blues, rock and jazz all arouse the Kundalini, it made it a cosmic thing for everyone, though of course I couldn't know that it was my help that was doing it. Even when I pulled the power back and the jam immediately fell apart, that was no way to know. Maybe I was just unconsciously anticipating the collapse.

Even so, I didn't let my doubts stop me. When I sent the energy, the band, if they had any room for spontaneity, would be brilliant, while if I didn't they often wound up just going through the motions. Simply put, I liked to get my money's worth and hated to waste my hearing on mediocrity. So I gave them the energy and didn't much care if I were helping or not. Until the time, that is, when I got all the proof I needed that I was indeed sending something significant. But the proof didn't come from the band.

The event occurred on 17 November 1988, when the Neville Brothers performed at Toad's Place, a rock club in New Haven. The Nevilles play a sort of rock-blues-reggae-cajun-voodoo-jazz, and the lead instrumentalist plays saxophone—soprano and tenor, mostly. Thus he was the focus of my efforts, and he looked as though he were responding directly. He acted as if he could feel the power coming from the crowd, for he seemed to soak it up when I sent it, search for it when I pulled it back, and once I'd settled into sending it continuously, our eye contact was frequent. And his performance was incredible, so much so that I soon reached a level where I was giving it to the band as a whole, and so theirs was, too. Or so it seemed, but who could tell? I could still have been projecting, and there was no way to ask without looking like a loony.

But it didn't matter. My head was in syncopated heaven and had given up on its desire for confirmation. My back, on the other hand, was tired and starting to hurt. I wanted to sit down but the place was packed, hundreds standing shoulder-to-shoulder across the dance floor, on the fringe of which I stood. But then when I looked around I saw I was standing next to a table and an empty chair. I could take not watching for a few minutes, so I started to sit down.

"I'm sorry, but there's someone sitting there," I heard from behind me. The speaker was a black gentleman, standing with a black lady. He was well-spoken and far better dressed than I was—elegant, not flashy. But I hurt, so…

"There's no one sitting in it," I countered, "and I'll be glad to get up as soon as they come back." He looked a bit pained, so I added, "I understand that you're saving it for yourself, but I'd just like to sit for a minute, and I'll get up whenever you want." He smiled tightly and nodded, then took his coat (which I hadn't noticed) off the back of the chair. As I sat down I apologized to his date. "I do appreciate it, and I'm awful sore." And sitting felt great.

About two minutes later a white youth, hardly twenty-one, approached the black gentleman, set his drink on the table, and asked if he had a light. The man lit a match, but the youth blew it out in "trying" to puff on his cigarette. I took more notice and right away saw something snide in his manner. The man gave him the matchbook, and the youth lit up with a cloud of smoke. He made a production out of handing the matches back, blew more smoke and started to talk over the 100 decibel band. I could see the gentleman grow more and more annoyed, while the youth was almost swaggering. The kid was harassing him because he was black, and the man could do nothing but put up with it.

Now I have read more than once (was it Crowley? Levi? Fortune?) that the safest way to reply to a curse is to make sure the curser knows you are aware of what he's doing, and then do him a service, no strings attached. This came to mind in a moment. In the next moment I spoke the word to send this creep a blast of the same stuff I'd been sending the sax player.

Within the same second the kid reached down for his full drink and raised it from the table. It slipped through his fingers. It fell— splopt!—at his feet. Astonishment crossed his face, then horror. He turned and fled into the crowd. The black man watched him leave, his face cloaked in wonder.

I looked away. In another minute I stood. I gestured to the chair and said, "Thank you very much." The man smiled as if he were delighted he had helped. I turned my attention back to the band and saw no more of him.

As for me, behind my straight face I was exultant. There was no doubt in my mind that I had made the little bigot drop his drink. A sax player might be brilliant as a matter of skill and will, but no one *tries* to drop a gin and tonic. When it happens in the same second, I'm satisfied.

So how did the energy do it? I would speculate it was a matter of disruption. Assuming that the root of all life is in the divine, behavior such as that of this little shit would be under the control of a demon—in this case a demon that feels good by lording over other people it sees as inferior. It takes its food from the bad feeling it evokes; the more adverse the reaction, the more satisfied it is. If it provokes an assault, it is in heaven, for then its "righteousness" is confirmed and it may reply in kind. So long as the response it spawns is negative, the demon is well-practiced, its routine smooth and certain.

Positive energy, on the other hand, is the one thing it has no use for. When it gets it, it is confused and its routine is disrupted. Its timing is destroyed, and in a confrontation, timing is everything. A tiny jolt was all it took to turn arrogance into embarrassment and make the problem run away.

There is one point here I need to stress: in no way did I have to force myself to think nice thoughts about this person before I blasted him. I thought he was pig dung, and I wanted him gone. So my feelings about him were irrelevant to the magick. What mattered was that the energy came in through my hairline and went out through my solar plexus, and the word I used to move it along and my visualization of it were identical to what I was sending to the band. It was an automatic action, and my emotions didn't matter.

So what, then, if my perception had been in error? Would my acrimony have found its mark? Not at all, for I wasn't sending acrimony. I was sending creative energy in the service of acrimony. If my displeasure had been misplaced and the youth were simply a young man devoid of both racial prejudice and social skills, he perforce would not have been acting under the influence of any demon. But if there had been no demon there, my positive energy would have had no malignancy to disrupt, only an innocent aura it could only strengthen. Perhaps the power would have enlightened the youth, causing him to see that it wasn't polite to engage strangers in conversation while a genius was playing the sax. Perhaps not. In either case my misplaced sense of justice would have found its weapon ineffective, and I hope I would have had the sense to leave it at that.

I should also remark that my state of mind during the concert was most certainly out of the ordinary, and this surely had an effect on my ability to do this work. The air was full of top-shelf music and I had taken sacraments like beer and such that are favored by those who worship the Snake at rock & roll shows. Thus my level of vitality was unusually heightened—into a state which I could not easily have duplicated within the next few days, or even until the Neville Brothers came back to town. But these are mere details of invocation, matters that may be disposed of through practice. It is the dynamic that is important. Once we are aware of it, we can work on its application through our own devices—without even risking hearing loss, if that be our wills.

But then I don't want to stop here, for in the months since this episode I have had a hint of one more way to disrupt those who need it. That is, this technique seems to work well at enhancing factionalism within groups. If one feeds energy to one faction while depriving the other, the result can be arrogant overreaching on the one hand and resentment on the other. By switching back and forth between them as circumstances dictate, one could create the same sort of wave function that knocks down suspension bridges in high winds. And this strategy also has a fail-safe to keep it from working against those who are essentially innocent. If the members of a group are all sincerely working toward a common goal, they'll hardly notice if some of their number seem to have more power than others. In fact, those who are fed the power will likely use it to help the others keep up. Thus this strategy would probably be most effective for disrupting entrenched political organizations—those whose members seek power to promote their own personal agendas and only tolerate their colleagues out of self-interest.

## II. Details of Application

Through continued use of this basic technique I came across a number of fine points of practice that can make the method a bit more precise and, perhaps, controllable—though the variables remain beyond exact calibration. Also, tricky questions arise concerning the possible abuse of the dynamic, fresh questions for the moralists of Chaos to contemplate.

We will address here questions of how the spiritual nature of the target personage affects the result, how the energy may be more effectively transmitted, and how the energy can cause specific effects through its focus onto specific chakras. All the data I present came from actual events. These were all at rock & roll shows, this for two reasons: they are usually pretty crowded, making the surreptitious manipulation of strangers both possible and desirable, and my consciousness is usually pretty highly exalted—from the *music*, of course.

My first example comes from a show I went to at a neighborhood tavern in February of 1989. Also in attendance was a party of five or six young adults, one of whom could only be described as a conspicuous thug. He reeked threat. He wore a black leather jacket; his hair was built up in a real 'do' with a plume in the back; and he was short and thick and primed to kick some butt—his eyes searching the bar for hostile stares. So I sent him some energy. Did he self-destruct? No, he settled down and had a good time. He quit strutting and glaring out daggers and started laughing with the women in his group. Probably the difference between him and the bigot in Part I was that his aggressive attitude was something he would willingly affirm—"I'm bad and I know I'm bad and you'll know it too if you want to make something out of it"—an honest Mars instead of a hypocritical self-inflation that has to tear others down to build itself up.

My next two examples have to do with how to make the energy work better. In the first I was at a show sending some energy to the band when I happened to think of a woman I had seen recently. My imagination conjured up some sexual excitement—excitement which both made my visualization of the energy more vivid and also seemed to make the band perk up with a flurry of power chords and such. So it can help if you have a pelvic engorgement. But then it isn't just how much energy you send, but how open your target is to receiving it. In general people who are confined by any sort of shell have difficulty taking it in. Improvisational musicians, for instance, show much more response to it than those who are locked into a practiced routine. Even with the Neville Brothers, when I went to see them a second time I was far less successful. I think this was because there was a video crew filming the show and the band had decided on a fixed sequence of numbers to fit the predetermined format—all death to the spontaneity the energy requires to express itself freely.

One sort of openness that may be deliberately manufactured is called, in the terminology of hypnosis, *rapport*. Rapport is obtained simply through a deliberate matching of perceptual and psychic states. One way is to match postures with your subject and say the word "one" every time he or she exhales. Or you can match postures and take turns describing what you see, hear and feel. "Now I see the light from the kitchen shining off the hair in front of my eyes." "Now I hear the children playing in the yard next door." "Now I feel my wrists resting against the insides of my thighs." And so on. Since you are in the same place and in the same positions, each statement will emphasize your shared psychic condition, reinforcing the natural link from your adjacent auras. If this is pursued with any seriousness, trance will occur very quickly and energy transfer will be as easy as sending it. Obviously this overt generation of rapport will only be possible when you are working openly with your subject, but in that case it is a superb method for creating a link. I should add, however, that care must be taken when one enters rapport with another sorcerer. He or she may have his or her own agenda.

Of course music is one perceptual circumstance that everyone attending a musical event will share, and so it can be said that everyone present is in rapport to a greater or lesser extent, which is probably one reason why this dynamic works so well at rock & roll shows.

My last three examples have to do with a refinement of the basic transfer—using visualization to send the energy to a specific chakra of the target personage in hopes of getting a specific effect appropriate to that chakra.

For the first, I was at a gig in a bar, sitting listening with a friend when an acquaintance of my friend stopped to talk on his way out. And talk. And talk. It was distracting and I could see my friend was only listening to be polite, or acting like he was listening, since the music was so loud it was hard to hear even someone who was shouting, which this person was. So I sent some energy to the base of his spine. He immediately straightened up and took his leave. Of course he'd been intending to go all along, but he hadn't, and then he was gone. It may have been coincidence, but it was timely enough for me.

My second example of this involves the same bar and the same band, but on a different night. One thing about this bar is that it is small and thus crowded whenever a band plays—with only about two feet between the end of the bar and the band's monitors and mike stands. This end of the bar is also the only way the help has to get behind it, so the traffic of bottles and glasses can get a bit touchy. On this occasion, however, things were even worse due to the presence of a person with a rather bizarre sense of camaraderie. He was tall and thin, but well-built, as if he spent much time on a weight machine, and he was with two other people—a fat guy only slightly shorter than he and a slightly built woman. But while his companions were acting normally, he was strutting around like a gamecock, engaging in all sorts of totally inappropriate rough play. He grabbed men he knew around the shoulders and shook them. He gripped the woman around the neck as if to choke her. He even wrestled with a barman as he tried to work three cases of bottled beer between the end of the bar and the band, risking a serious accident. He was clearly wound up so tight that just sending him energy could cause him to pop. But it was also clear that the woman wanted to dance. So I sent some energy to his groin, hoping to make him notice her. So did he dance? No. He got into a deep, soulful conversation with the fat guy, who I noticed was wearing a heavy leather belt with a thick, silver chain hanging from the left side. And the thin guy had on a heavy leather belt with a large bunch of keys hanging from the right side. So you learn something new every day. But then this variation was okay by me, for he calmed right down and I didn't see him wrestle anyone else for the rest of the night.

For my last example I offer my most frivolous use of this dynamic, and thus also the most morally dubious. It was again a case of same place, same band, different night. I was sitting at a table with some friends. At a table across the aisle were two couples. Though one of the men was a conspicuous fan of the music, the other clearly felt precisely the opposite. He was of late middle age, wearing a tan suit and a tie, sitting rigidly erect with a very stern expression—a Jeremiah in Babylon for sure. He was only there for the others' sake and did not approve. So I sent a blast to the base of his spine. For a moment he weakened, his fingers beginning to tap out the rhythm on his knee. But then he caught hold of himself, clamped his arms across his chest, and thus restrained his errant digits. I didn't know whether to laugh or cry, and for a moment thought of redoubling my efforts. But then I remembered the third enemy of a man of knowledge and, wary of the threat, pulled the energy back and endeavored to mind my own business.

In his *Teachings of don Juan*, Carlos Castaneda quotes don Juan as saying that the four enemies of a man of knowledge are fear, clarity, power and old age. Fear is failure, of course, and so a clear enough obstacle. Clarity comes when one defies fear, but if one interprets it as Truth, it blinds one and one's progress stops. If the sorcerer can defy clarity, though, he will reach a point when he realizes that this clarity is a veil of certainty that hides the shifting currents of power beneath it. Once a sorcerer can recognize these currents, he can manipulate them to do whatever he wants. And thus he encounters his (or her) third enemy, which is power.

Don Juan stresses that power is both our most powerful enemy and also the easiest to give in to, for it gives one mastery over one's fellows. Blinded by this mastery, the sorcerer will scarcely notice as it gains dominance over him, until—without him realizing it—power defeats him. "His enemy will have turned him into a cruel, capricious man." (p. 81)

According to don Juan, the way to defeat power is to defy it, just as one must defy fear and clarity. The sorcerer must always be aware "that the power he has seemingly conquered is in reality never his." (p. 82) In Thelemic terms, we have "no right but to do our wills," without "lust of result," but if we do that, "no other can say nay." Obviously giving nervous breakdowns to strangers in upper-level management, while jolly good fun, is no part of my will, and to indulge in it would only make me a psychic bully. And so I refrained, and thanked Castaneda for the warning. Regardless of the reality of don Juan, his books are full of good stuff. You just have to try it yourself and see.

## III. Eucharists

Since I wrote Part II of "Sending Power to Help and Hurt" for *Chaos International* no. 8, I have had the edifying experience of hearing a friend who was on the receiving end of the energy tell me what it was like. My friend broached the subject during an intermission in a performance of his rock & roll band, when he asked me if I perhaps thought that things were extremely weird that evening. I replied that yes, I did indeed, but then I always tried to make things as weird as possible, and sometimes erred by making them weirder than they actually were. He mulled that one over for a moment, and then simply stated that be that as it may, they were grateful for all the positive energy they could get. Then he went to the bar to get more beer.

Now this for me seemed a bit of a breakthrough. I've had two other people tell me that they felt energy that I had sent in this way, but they're both magicians themselves and knew I was sending it—heard me chant the words—the idea being that it would help us accomplish specific magickal purposes. But my musician friend was giving me my first unsolicited confirmation, and he isn't concerned with magick at all. I had given him a copy of "Sending Power I" (*C.I.* 6) over a year earlier, so he knew what I thought I could do, but in all the times I'd used it on his band, I'd never mentioned I was doing it, figuring that if I asked if he'd felt anything, he'd just say that he supposed he did—this so I wouldn't feel bad. But here he was volunteering the experience with no encouragement from me, and this obviously required further investigation. So the next day I drove over for a visit and asked what the reception of positive energy had felt like. He replied that it had made him feel as if he could do no wrong. Since my friend plays electric mandolin—where speed rather than hesitation is the prime virtue—this was obviously a good feeling to get. So I asked where he felt it. Was it in his fingers? No, he hardly ever noticed his fingers. Head and spine, then? He guessed so. So now I just send it to his image in my mind's eye, and also into my image of the music itself.

Of course the main drawback of this technique is that you can't use it to give power directly to yourself. It comes in at the hairline, so it's free power, but if it doesn't go out the solar plexus, there's no telling what damage it might do. But even if we can't pump the power of the Cosmic One directly into our auras, we can still get it for ourselves, with results that are striking. The method for doing this is the charging and consumption of the eucharist.

Crowley's definition of the eucharist in *Magick in Theory and Practice* is most useful: "Take a substance symbolic of the whole course of nature, make it God, and consume it." (p. 179) This "making God" has traditionally been done by means of a ritual exaltation of the substance, but may also be accomplished with great efficiency by means of the "Sending Power" dynamic, the eucharistic substance being a worthwhile substitute for a rock & roll musician—and easier to eat, too!

Which substance should we choose, then? I have concentrated on two: water from a power spot, and my own semen.

In the section on exorcism in the chapter "Rites of Chaos" in his book *Psychonaut*, Peter J. Carroll remarks that water is "possessed of a certain delicate structure which is very sensitive to heat, radiation, and psychic ambiance. It will receive a psychic charge readily, but will dissipate it equally readily." From this follows the well-known difficulty of working magick across running water, it being prone to absorb and thus diminish the forces sent over it. But such ready absorption is just what we require of our eucharistic medium, and since we're planning on its immediate consumption, it doesn't matter if it lacks the capacity to hold the power for long. In fact, since it's better to sweep the power into our belly chakras before we swallow, such a tenuous attachment is an advantage, allowing our Light to grab the power without undue effort. And water has the additional benefit of being notably easy to get down.

Of course if the water comes out of a location known to be a power spot, so much the better. It has power even before one rams more into it, and by being thus suffused with power, it seems all the more capable of absorbing an additional charge. It is possible, however, that water from an undistinguished source could be consecrated before being charged, perhaps by dissolving in it some salts that had been prepared as a talisman.

Now for most of the four years that I've used the water from this spot, I've simply charged and then drunk it, but in the past year I've found a way to amplify the energy that I've given it. Rather than just send in the energy that comes in from beyond the hairline chakra, before I open any charkas I first assume the god-form of Ra-Hoor-Khuit—head of a hawk crowned with the sun, the sun itself providing the energy that I send.[8] Being a Thelemite, this is obviously a potent form for me to assume, and anyway, the spot from whence my water comes is beloved of hawks, for I have seen them as I climbed the rock to obtain it.

Working from this same Thelemic orientation, before I consume my eucharists I generally assume the form of Hoor-paar-

---

[8] And not just for charging eucharists. High-energy rock bands seem to love him. It was after I had begun taking the form of Ra-Hoor that my friend the mandolin player first remarked upon the energy I was sending him.

kraat. As a totally passive Babe in an Egg, I find I can sweep the power from my mouth into my belly chakra much more easily than I can when I am in my normal form. When the charge is a strong one, this is an important consideration.

Semen is obviously a more intrinsically potent medium than water, capable of holding a much stronger charge. The disadvantage of using it is that the very act of producing it can be rather draining, making it difficult to charge with this dynamic, and quite impossible to assume a god-form in any convincing manner. The way I get around this is to charge a quantity of water beforehand, wrap its vessel in black cloth to guard against accidental discharge, and then manufacture the elixir. Then I drink the water, and under its vivifying influence charge the elixir and then consume it. If I have prepared myself by indulging in an adequate worship of the Snake ("who giveth Knowledge & Delight"), this combination can be strikingly effective. The results may not be all that apparent at first, but upon retiring they can be extremely disturbing. On one occasion the area around my belly chakra went into painless spasms, which only stopped after I drained off some of the power by using it to fill my whole body with healing energy. (I didn't think I was sick, but I had to use it for something.) Another time I found that I had a sexual engorgement that could not be relieved in the usual way, for its reappearance after orgasm was immediate. So I sent it up my spine instead, and as I drifted off to sleep it seemed as if my Serpent had turned into concrete, so hard and heavy was the energy there.

It is important that I note that the use of sexual fluids in magick should not be begun lightly, and requires a commitment to the discipline of *chastity*. This caution was first stated by Aleister Crowley in his "secret" instructions to the O.T.O.—especially in *Liber Agape*. Chastity might be most concisely defined as the treatment of sexual fluids as vehicles of power that may be either dedicated to a purpose (e.g., conjuration, the love of Nuit, the getting of children) or else reabsorbed, but which must never be promiscuously wasted. By submitting ourselves to this discipline we accumulate power that would otherwise be discarded, focus our discharge of power so it reinforces our wills, and prevent the appropriation of our power by spirits domestic and foreign who would suck it up to promote their own agendas and hence—perforce—thwart ours.

One final remark: I've found it advisable to have a word to cut off the flow of power into the target—whether person or eucharist—after I've finished sending it and before I pull it back. It is always better to keep one's aura discrete—self-contained and separate—for as Paracelsus tells us, indistinct auras have a susceptibility to whatever stresses the environment contains. Also, it is less disruptive to the target to have the flow of power disengaged before it is withdrawn.

This is an adaptation of a three-part sequence that appeared in *Chaos International* nos. 6, 8 and 11, London, 1989, 1990 and 1991.

# Power Spots:
# Their Discovery and Use

Modern magick—the occult theory and practice of Levi and Mathers, Crowley and Spare, Regardie and Grant—has been for the most part an affair of the individual psyche. According to their up-to-date view, the powers for sorcery are to be found within the consciousness or unconsciousness of each magician. The attainment of this perspective was an essential stage in the evolution of magick, for there surely is omnipotence at the source of our souls, but it is a very recent development, much at variance with the sorcerous belief of the preceding 50,000 years. Before the psychological enlightenment of the last few centuries, the powers of sorcery were seen as living 'outside' the sorcerer—as gods, spirits and demons that existed on their own and only occasionally blessed, possessed or were conjured by specific men and women. While it may seem more reasonable to internalize these forces, saying they are powers of mind or even (when there are paranormal displays) supermind, we would be sinfully restrictive if we simply rejected the notion of spiritual power as existing independently of biological consciousness. Fidelity to the Neither-Neither requires that we examine the opposite perspective—that the natural world is full of powers unconnected to animal consciousness but nonetheless available to it, if only we be fluid enough to catch them. Some of these powers are so vast that they are easily accessible, but others are discrete and concentrated, spiritual vents in the surface of the earth. By finding these and connecting to their flow, the sorcerer may use them to supplement his or her energy, or even to provide a boost into new levels of understanding. But we must voice a caution here. Power can pour out of a location in space, but may also be sucked down into it. Thus for an individual wizard a spot may be beneficial or malign, depending on its particular dynamics. And there is some evidence that good and bad spots come in pairs—that if you find a good one, there will be a bad one nearby, and vice-versa. I have encountered this in my own experience, and in *Teachings*, Carlos Castaneda has don Juan explaining that the good was called "the *sitio*" and the bad "the enemy," that the good "created superior strength" while the bad "weakened a man and could even cause his death."

To begin, it would seem prudent to make a distinction between two very different types of spot. The first is the sort that places the wizard where power is readily accessible, as the ocean is to a beach. The second is the sort of place that serves as a source of power in itself, as a spring is a source of water, and a volcano of lava. The first type is easier to recognize; the second is both harder to find and harder to handle once found, but with enormous potential for change.

With the first type, then, the wizard simply decides to get in touch with a specific type of power and then looks for a place that will put him there. If we want to invoke the Earth, any cave or mine or narrow leafy valley will suffice. To adore Our Lady Nuit, any high crag or open field will bring us to her. To call on powers of Moon and Sea, a spit of land is best—a solid place that needs no sailing but which may shudder underfoot as the powers of storm and tide surge about it. Dion Fortune's *The Sea Priestess* gives a good account of the use of such a place.

Or perhaps for the Moon a wooded island would do as well, solitary in a vast marsh whose tide-flooded grasses glisten in her silver light.

In any event, places such as these mostly just need finding, which can be a sorcerous task indeed if one lives in a city or even in a built-up suburb. Open space is essential, simply so one can make a joyful noise unto the Lord without having the neighbors call the police. Roads are alright in their place, and of course crossroads are traditionally *the spot* to conjure on. But then in tradition there were no automobiles or street lighting, so perhaps paths crossing in deep woods would be more practical. Other than that, one needs merely to work out of the sight of roads, so as not to be interrupted by passers-by. At least in the United States, the first principle of police behavior is that they never get out of their cars unless they are investigating a complaint. If you stay both unavailable and inconspicuous, they'll never notice you.

Once the wizard has become familiar with an area and accustomed to doing his work out-of-doors, he is in a position to search out spots of the second sort—those where the location itself coincides with a critical nexus in the dynamics of planetary power. This is not meant to sound terribly cosmic. There are surely millions of such spots scattered across the surface of the globe—pores in the skin of our Mother. But an area of, say, a hundred square feet can be tough to find in five square miles of rough country. We need to use all the means at our command—rational and occult—to distinguish the truly numinous from the merely spectacular. Three that immediately come to mind are the recognition of incongruous terrain, omens, and clairvoyance.

Incongruous terrain is the easiest way to take notice of a spot. If there is nothing but salt marsh and delta islands for miles, and you find an outcropping of bedrock, it would seem wise to investigate it magickally. If you know an open heath where there stands, for no apparent reason, a grove of ancient oaks, try doing some magick there. If you do your work atop a ridge of rock, hundreds of feet above the water table, and if at the edge of a high cliff you find a spring, perhaps there is power welling up with the water. And perhaps the water is itself infused with power. The proof of that is in the drinking.

The reader may wonder here what makes such incongruity holy, and I answer that to presume that it may be is a pragmatic application of that essential Hermetic dictum: "What is below is like that which is above, and what is above is like that which is below, to accomplish the miracles of the One Thing." In other words, when the material features of a location in space are strange and out of place, the spiritual features may well be also, perhaps in an analogous way. Of course a skeptic might reply that if a spring has power, the Mississippi should have an infinitely greater quantity, and yet St. Louis is hardly a Mecca for sorcerers, or Vicksburg, either. This is all quite true, but it misses the essence, which is *intensity*. A great river's power is grand and overspreading, so diffuse that its field can encompass its whole watershed. There is no contrast between one point and the next, and so there is no potential. And the same could be said for a region of many springs, for there would be an overspreading state of balance in that space, too. But when there is just one spring on a whole mountain, or one rock sticking up out of acres of grassy muck, then we can reasonably look for an analogous tension on the planes above. If our magick confirms it, then we have a source of power for the taking, assuming it is the sort of power we need to do what we need to do. And there are a number of different ways that power can flow. While one spot may seem to be a fountain of power—perfect for circulation of the Light and overall enhancement of one's aura—another may be best suited for planting power after a conjuration, as if it were a window into the causal plane. On the other hand, a spot may be malign, acting as a whirlpool sucking away the vitality of any auras so ignorant that they expose themselves to it. Hence you should not begin to use a spot just because it feels weird. If it's not nice-weird, leave it alone.

Omens are harder to work at than the search for the random odd landscape, simply because they must come of themselves, but they're easier to use if only you have the power to notice them. And yet there are also those omens that seem more like a kick in the head, those that must be interpreted as omens if you are to believe in omens at all, and of course if you don't you're not likely to be out looking for power spots.

For instance, I can recall a time when a friend and I were occupied with doing ritual readings of *Liber AL vel Legis* on the top of a high hill, the Body of our Lady Nuit above us, the glorious world her sister—adorned with ten thousand lights—spread out beneath her soft feet. One night I was reading along when we were impaled on the blue-white beam of a searchlight, this attached to a fire engine idling on a street a half mile away. The park was closed, you see, and we had lit a fire, which was not permitted. So we ran away and snuck home without getting popped, but just barely. The omen, however, came right at the beginning, for the last line I read before the spotlight hit was:

> Now this mystery of the letters is done, and I want to go on to the holier place. (III: 48)

It was clear Ra-Hoor disapproved of our location and wanted us to find a new one. Winter was coming so we had to have fires, but that meant the top of the hill was out of the question. Under the omen's command we searched for a more sheltered spot and found one that in its way was more numinous than the one with the awesome view. The skeptic can object that it was inevitable that we would be discovered and forced off the peak, but that the discovery should be imposed just as I was reading that one verse is a superb statement by Ra-Hoor. To dismiss such exquisite timing as mere coincidence is to dismiss all Magick, and to forfeit its power.

Of course we don't have to wait and be surprised by omens; we can also go looking for them, perhaps by trekking into open country with the intent of following the first hawk we see, or fox, or whatever other animal we associate with power. Or perhaps it will be a shape in the clouds, or a particular species of plant. It's up to the individual, of course. But regardless of specific procedure, if you wander about with the sole purpose of finding power, you will as often as not obtain significant results. Even if at the beginning we find only small powers, with small power we may prepare ourselves for greater power, and so on until we find all we need. The important thing is to start.

This sort of wandering about looking for power is also a great way to encourage clairvoyance, which, when developed, is also an effective tool for finding power spots. By clairvoyance I mean both the ability to travel into the astral and also that of directly perceiving the power of things—their auras, as it were. Astral projection can give us information about a stretch of country as well as it can about anything else, and we can even do it in the field if we can find a place that's lonely enough. More immediate, though, is the clairvoyance that happens when a wizard gets a feeling for a spot, or can see the shape and color of its aura—Light hovering about the elements of the landscape and even (if he can shift his eyes correctly) within them.

And yet it is not so easy to see, especially if we are obliged by habits of thought to think about what we are looking at, or are worried about how 'valid' what we see might be. Seeing auras might be regarded as a sort of wide-awake Death Posture, the aura perceived in half-light on a separate screen in the mind's eye. And yet if we can shift our attentions to it, it grows more dominant, more accurate, as real as the normal way of seeing things. It's a matter of personal power, mostly, and making our persons accessible to power is what finding power spots is all about. So finding them through their Light is an advanced technique, most likely to be perfected after the need for it has diminished. Like all magic power, it may be seen as the reward of doing well what it helps us to do, even though we don't yet have it. When it almost seems as if we can do without it, it comes of itself, and reveals a new world.

Words fail.

First published in *Vitriol* no. 1, Leeds, 1987.

# Some Considerations on the Absorption and Use of Alien Energy

The trouble with vampirism is that the energy isn't yours. Now don't get me wrong; feeding on other people's power is a rush. An orgasmic surge that overwhelms you with a pleasure that won't quit, it is the most striking evidence for the objective existence of "vital force" that I have ever encountered. Nor am I here presenting any moral arguments against theft. There are plenty of people who are so undisciplined that they shed their energy wherever they go, so it's easy enough to suck it up before they miss it and come back to look for it. There are even some who enjoy the oblivion of the Sleep of Death that follows being fed upon, and will subtly encourage you to eat your fill, or even thrust their energy upon you so forcefully that you must either feed upon it or else fight it off (which is how I became acquainted with this dynamic). And if you are willing to be a bit more ethically fuzzy (which is probably needful once you find your appetite), you will discover ways to make yourself *attractive*, in one way or another serving as bait for other people's desires, the type of energy you obtain depending on the type of bait it is your predilection to be. You should serve as a mirror for your victim's desires, projecting back an image of what it is that he or she wants, driving his or her need to an ever higher pitch until he or she cannot help but indulge in release. When the release comes, the energy should be palpable, and then may be taken in through the various arts of subtle manipulation. If you feel the energy in your groin, draw it up your spine and reabsorb it later as the sacrament spawned upon sexual self-stimulation. If you feel it in one of your other centers, wheel it directly into your belly chakra.

Whatever you do, don't indulge in any sort of spending, sexual or otherwise. Then you won't be absorbing energy but rather exchanging it, something no self-respecting vampire would consider doing. There's no satiety in that, and the risk of an honest relationship—even affection or love—will be considerable.

The classic approach to vampirism is of course the sexual, and in Chapter XVIII of his *De Arte Magica*, Aleister Crowley hints at the method when he says the vampire uses his body, "most usually the mouth," to drain his victim, "without himself entering in any other way into the matter." Which is to say, by performing oral sex on the victim, the vampire can cause him or her to expend copious quantities of energy in orgasm, and an elixir also, both of which may be absorbed by the vampire without the vampire needing to emit any power at all. That's the archetype, but it can be applied to types of power other than the sexual.

The problem is not thus one of getting the energy; the problem is assimilating it once it is absorbed. Again, it isn't yours, no more than the victim's pants are yours. Which is to say, it won't fit you, and will need to be recut and resewn if it is to do so. The energy consumed will bring with it the victim's temperament both physical and mental, his or her view of the world, his or her demons and spirits, his or her whole relationship with reality. This is not an insurmountable obstacle. If the victim was essentially active and you are sedentary, you must simply maintain your level of relaxation in spite of the surge of momentum you must disregard to do so. But the less physical aspects of the power—mental, emotional, spiritual—will be more difficult to discern and hence more difficult to recognize as needing adaptation. Of course you may carry out programs of introspection and astral research after each feeding, using magickal methods to reorient any alien tendencies so they mesh with your own momentum. But I suspect it is a very rare vampire who has the initiative or discipline to do this to the extent required. And if it isn't done, the victim's karmic momentum will be assimilated along with his or her energy, muddling the vampire's direction and corrupting his or her will. The vampire will acquire lots of energy, but with all its directional vectors mixed. Thus it will be only "being," with no sort of "going" to it at all—dynamic force corrupted to serve mere "existence." The process that you are will bog down in indeterminacy and stop.

In all this I need to emphasize the distinction between the energy theft of vampirism and the free exchange typical of a sexual or even a commercial relationship. Again, the crux of the vampyric process is that the vampire does not spend. He or she absorbs energy but never emits it—neither as orgasm nor affection nor value nor any other impetus except the desire for more energy and the pleasure it brings. When one is in a normal relationship, on the other hand, one gives and takes energy freely, and the more free the exchange, the more intertwined will be the lives of the participants. Another point is that energy freely exchanged finds its way home eventually, while energy deliberately consumed is gone forever. It and its karma also are absorbed, never to return again.

Of course the vampire must contend with the intertwining of lives as much as the lover, for the vampire's victims' power will serve to link the vampire to them. In fact, they will form a sort of "stable," much in the way certain cinematic directors (e.g., Woody Allen, John Waters) maintain stables of actors that they repeatedly use in their films. These victims will hang around until they catch on to the dynamic of their relationship with the vampire, then flee with whatever portion of their energy they are able to salvage.

The result of all this is the bloated vampire, too satiated with other people's power to assert the momentum of his or her own, his or her only desire the acquisition of more energy (for the rush attendant to its absorption as much as any will toward self-aggrandizement), attended by his or her current swarm of acolytes, vilified by those who have survived to run away.

And there will also be those former victims who have become aware of the dynamic and decide to try it for themselves. To be fed upon by a vampire tends to sensitize one to the processes of energy exchange, so if one has a modicum of talent in this direction, and a taste for strong pleasures, one may choose to follow one's "mentor" in that path, and begin oneself to feed.

It's not an easy option to turn down. Already sufficient in one's own power, one confronts the opportunity of accessing a seemingly endless supply with which to supplement it, so much power that immortality itself must be the reward. Of course there's no way one could demonstrate that without committing oneself to the vampire life, but even if one chose to, unless one were a truly masterful astral craftsman the chance for immortality would necessarily be a mirage. Unless the alien force is perfectly assimilated, it will corrupt physical health as surely as it corrupts spiritual destiny. During my magickal career I have met two people who I strongly suspect follow the vampire path; both are physical wrecks. And as a magickal friend advised me during the conversation wherein she persuaded me to reject the vampyric option, "There's energy all over the place. You don't need to get it from other people." But if you do get it from other people, you will likely lose the fine edge of discernment you need to tap the other sources. Bloated with the strong brew of other people's life force, why bother to look for anything less full-bodied?

But then where are these more subtle, albeit ubiquitous, sources of power? Well, they're wherever you can bring it to bay. There's power in the wind, in the trees, in the sea. It's in the building you work in, the road you drive on, and in the club where you hear your rock & roll. You just have to meet it on its own ground, recognize it for what it is, and bind it to your purpose.

What I speak of here are the elementals that are associated with specific physical locations and objects in space. My essential supposition is that any discrete physical entity will have a discrete aetheric counterpart that may be managed with sorcerous technique. By learning this elemental's True Name and binding it—as if it were a spirit on the astral—you can perceive and distinguish its various energies and access them for your own use.

In my experience, elementals' True Names are barbarous ones. I learn the Name through consultation with my Holy Guardian

Angel, without whose assistance I would find this technique difficult indeed to apply. I do the binding with the "Hear Me, and make all Spirits subject unto Me…" charge from Crowley's "Preliminary Invocation" in the *Goetia*. In my own work I have always done this meeting and binding while in waking consciousness, banishing and centering in imagination and then calling up the HGA for a quick naming. So astral projection isn't necessary, though I have found the process seems clearer if I have been sanctified by appropriate Sacraments of the Snake.

The binding of the elemental allows you to access and manipulate its energies and also to prevent it from accessing and manipulating yours—which is to say, possessing you. It does not mean you will be able to control the physical behavior of the physical thing the elemental is associated with. For one thing, so much of what happens to it is determined by outside forces. Wood rots because it gets rained on, and a rapport with your house won't constrain the cloud spirits. For another, physical inertia must be overcome, and it will always be considerable. So try using elementals to cause physical change if you like, but that's not what I'm offering here.

The subject of possession is pertinent to this type of magick, simply because one must stand in the very midst of the elemental's domain while one conjures and binds it, and also later whenever one manipulates its power. Thus it is imperative that you banish, and then center and consecrate yourself, before beginning, and use a Word of Separation upon departing, after which you should banish and center again. Of course if you can do this within a consecrated circle, all the better, but that doesn't work very well if the location in question is your place of employment or the middle of the Thames. So it's best if you've developed your aura to the extent that you can carry your circle around with you all the time. If you haven't, this is not a magick I would recommend doing.

On the other hand, I should note that some locations will be more difficult to bind than others. When I bound the elemental associated with what men call Long Island Sound (a body of water about 15 miles wide and a hundred miles long), it was as if it were utterly indifferent to the act, which seemed more a formality than anything else. But when I bound the elemental of a local tavern, it was as hard as binding a deeply set demon. The difference is that the tavern needs human attention to survive, while the Sound will be there until the oceans recede, or until the glaciers return to fill it with earth and stone.

This doesn't mean I could have dispensed with binding the Sound's elemental or that I don't need to center myself before swimming in it. Even if an elemental is entirely benevolent, one still needs to affirm one's discrete existence before calling it up and immersing oneself in it. In the case of the Sound, the elemental is essentially indifferent to human attention, so there is little cause for concern. Even so, I still take pains to respect it. I always thank it before separating and banishing, and littering or any pollution of the water is anathema to me.

Now at this point some readers may ask, "Why bother to call up the elemental of a large body of water?" Well, consider the aspects of its power. It seeks and *always* attains its own level, which is to say, it does its will. It opposes and vanquishes over time all attempts to interfere with this attainment, its turbulent motion capable of dissolving all obstruction. These are worthwhile aspects of power to develop, and I have found that by requesting a specific one before swimming, then chanting the Name as a mantra as I do so, I am able to absorb a modicum of power each time. The most striking results have come after requesting the power to dissolve obstructions, for it has greatly helped my ongoing effort to open the channels of my subtle anatomy, especially the critical nexus at the base of my spine.

So much for inland seas. At the other end of the spectrum we have things like local taverns, places of employment, and other habitations of men. Harder to bind and more apt to possess, why bother to deal with them? Again, it is for the support they are able to give us. In the case of the tavern, I met and bound its elemental in an attempt to boost the energy level of my favorite rock & roll band. Readers of *Chaos International* will recall that previously I did this by means of the dynamic described in "Sending Power to

Help and Hurt." But that method is problematic in two ways. It requires extreme breathing, which is quite troublesome when a room is full of tobacco smoke, and it's a lot of work. Of course it is free power, but it's free in the same sense that dirt is free. If you want it, you still have to dig it up and haul it to where you need it to be. Sick of acting like a smoke-clogged power pump, I decided to try to cause the venue itself to provide the support.

Naturally the results remain subjective, but to my way of listening the method seems to work fairly well. You simply call up the elemental and ask it to assist the musicians as they play, then intone the name as a mantra as they do so. The result seems to be that they make music with more unity, confidence and enthusiasm than they often do otherwise. I also tried this with a name act in a football stadium. It was raining and the crowd was wet and unsupportive, including myself, and I wasn't about to pump power for them. I mean, I paid $31.00 to have them do the work! In any event, the first set was crushingly lackluster, so during the break I found the name of the place and asked its assistance. Everyone I spoke to agreed the second set was brilliant.

Now I admit this last anecdote may make me seem somewhat megalomaniacal, and to that I can only reply: *try it yourself!* My only claim is that the technique is worth using. Any competent mage should be able to apply it as well as I. And besides, there was one fact about the performance that supports my supposition of an effective interference. After I'd asked the elemental's assistance, it was the drums and bass that flourished, pushing and kicking the guitars and keyboards into musical excellence. I see the reason for this in the structure of the stadium itself. It is a massive concrete pile with seats for about 80,000 people, built on a marsh so probably having foundations on caissons sunk to bedrock. Thus it clearly has a very low frequency of vibration, and so it is likely its elemental would be able to give the lower instruments more help than the higher. On the other hand, the tavern I mentioned is one story high and built of cinderblock, so its elemental would be able to give the higher instruments more support.

Again, try it yourself and discover your own parameters.

The crux, then, for this aspect of the method is that the elemental of a place can be called in to support the humans who inhabit it, whether these people are aware of what you are doing or not. This could be applied to anything from your sister in the hospital to your client at the advertising agency—or to yourself as a jobseeker, about to apply at the office tower of your dreams. Or consider getting the assistance of the British Library before beginning to search for an obscure text. Nor need you have any concern about exploiting the elemental, since giving its human occupants a boost is as much to its advantage as it is to the occupants'. After all, if the elemental of a tavern helps a band be brilliant, it'll help pack in the customers, pay the mortgage, and keep the place from being torn down to build a shopping mall. It's a symbiotic relationship, no sort of parasitism at all.

Now though this about sums up my experience with elementals thus far, there are two other aspects of the dynamic that come to mind. I haven't tried either of them, but they seem intriguing, so I'll offer them up in case someone else would like to. And these are 1.) acquiring luck in gambling, and 2.) combat magick.

1) As I said earlier, I have no reason to suspect that binding an elemental should enable the magician to influence the physical behavior of its physical domain. Thus one could not expect that the favor of the elemental of a casino would grant luck in the realm of spinning wheels and falling dice. But perhaps the favor of a race-track could inspire one's chosen horse to run faster, or the favor of a stadium could cause one's football team to play with greater courage and skill. The only downside to success that I can see here is one of karma. Since the betting at such contests is parimutuel, your success would be at the expense of the other bettors, not the spiritually non-existent "Limited Liability Corporation" that would be the loser in the case of a casino.

2) The application of this method to combat magick is more intriguing, with implications interpersonal, historical, commercial and political. As I see it, the crux of this should be that if one has an opponent one wants to be rid of, one can simply turn all the places one shares with the person against the person. If successful,

it would serve to get the opponent out of one's life without risking the retribution consequent to launching a whammy at his or her own person. Whether your opponent in Parliament, your competitor at the electronics fair, your brutal husband, or your supervisor at Intergalactic Megaglom, Ltd., you would simply name and bind the elemental of the place you share and adjure the spirit to get the person out of there.

Now I must again admit that I personally have never tried to use elementals in combat magick, but there is historical precedent for it, passed down by the late 4th century Latin writer Macrobius. He devotes the ninth chapter of the third book of his *Saturnalia* to an explanation of how the Romans of the Republic applied this approach to war. They worked on the assumption that every city has a tutelary deity, so whenever they put a city under siege, they would evoke this spirit and conjure it to betray the inhabitants. The Romans did this both to make the city fall more easily and also so the god would be magickally appeased and so disinclined to inflict any divine retribution upon them. At the conclusion of this conjuration, living victims would be slaughtered in the bloody sacrifice and their entrails inspected for omens concerning the success of the rite.

It is the last sentence of the conjuration—"if ye shall so have done, I vow to you temples and solemn games" (p. 218)—that seems especially pertinent to combat magick, and even to elemental magick in general. The crux is that you're conjuring the spirit to take your part in a dispute with one of the other humans who inhabit its physical location. Helping you doesn't do it any good, and the strife may ultimately be to its detriment. So it seems reasonable to reward its favor with sacrifice. For the Romans this was a pact in the form of a promise of temples and solemn games. A modern magician may find that merely burning incense during a simple rite would be adequate. In these spiritless times, most elementals of man-made structures are starved for attention, so even the most basic acknowledgement of their existence could gain their favor. On the other hand, we can easily imagine two magicians going to extreme lengths to win the favor of an elemental in a contest over who will expel the other from their common space. But then does an elemental, once bound, stay loyal? If so, it could be a case of the winner being the first one out of the gate, leading (in a time of bad blood) to an inordinate number of preemptive bindings. Hardly a splendid prospect.

To close I'd like to remark upon one further occasion when sacrifice might be warranted. That is, when the place in question is a weak one, and thus the elemental incapable of assisting in much of anything. So it might be reasonable to do magick to build up its power. Fed on your sacrifices, the place would become as if it were a talisman—a Magickal Citadel on the Planes of Consequence, even if only a hovel on a wasteland to the eyes of men.

First published in *Chaos International* no. 16, London, 1994.

# Omens

Although omens have a dynamic similar to divination, they differ in that they are spontaneous. While divination with Tarot, I Ching or the runes is simply the use of a random symbol generator to solicit an omen, we can still use the mechanism anytime we like, and only the pertinence of the answers can indicate whether our solicitations are successful or not. But omens come when they come, and if we strive to see them when they aren't there, we only look ridiculous. A true omen can't be searched out, but manifests more like a kick in the head.

Sometimes omens are indicative of vast historical currents. Since these address public affairs, they will generally be public displays and so will often be reported in the media. Here is the headline for such a report, distributed by the Knight-Rider syndicate and printed in the New Haven *Register* of Tuesday, 8 November 1994, the day of the midterm elections, concerning an event that occurred the previous day:

## Crash kills 4 slowed by motorcade

The pile-up occurred on Interstate 75 in Mundy Township, Michigan, when President Bill Clinton's passing motorcade stopped traffic and a tractor-trailer smashed into it. The story explains that the truck had broadsided a car that had cut in front of it in order to drive across the median strip, this apparently in an attempt to avoid the congestion by making a U-turn. This started a chain reaction that took out six other vehicles. Several caught on fire, including two of the three new Saturn cars the truck was hauling. The truck driver survived, but the police did not say if he would be charged with any crime. The President had been on his way to address a crowd at the University of Michigan-Flint.

And of course the news for Tuesday was that President Bill Clinton's political party had suffered a flaming crack-up at the polls, and he was now going to have to deal with Republican majorities in both houses of Congress.

This accident was thus a perfect example of an ominous event, classic in its link to its subject, in its timing, and in the explicit character of its message. The link to the President was intimate because his presence caused it, but only in the most detached sense, so there's no way it can be seen as any kind of Freudian slip. Traffic stops for lots of reasons—construction, accidents up the road, tolls—and when there are pile-ups then, it is no omen. But the timing here was so precise. It was the day before the election and because the Top Democrat was making a campaign stop, four people were incinerated in a lake of fire. So of course the Democrats lost both houses.

The details of the story also carry meaning. Four people were killed, and four is the number of completion and stability. This to me emphasizes that the old Congressional status quo is finished and destroyed. Also, the cars the truck was hauling were Saturns, and Saturn is the planet of limit, form and Fate, again stressing that this political shift is no triviality. On the other hand, I see no indication here that a new Republican dynasty will result. It was a lake of fire, not a truckload of cantaloupes spilled out for anyone to gather. Besides, the driver of the car the truck broadsided was trying to make a U-turn himself, so a political U-turn is not likely to solve it. Something more creative is obviously required, and I doubt the Republicans have it in them.

Another detail is that the truck driver survived, just as Bill Clinton is still in office. And if the Republicans make a mess of it, he could well be re-elected in 1996—probably running on his ability to roll with the punches and turn disaster to good account. But that's still up in the air. After all, the police hadn't yet decided if the truck driver was at fault.[9]

So much for the portentous extreme. At the other end of the spectrum are omens that occur subtly to one's own person. You may be thinking mean thoughts about your sweetie when a crow starts cawing right overhead—the first crow you've heard all day. The message here would obviously be an admonition not to indulge in infantile crap. Of course this ominous event is tiny compared to Clinton's portent, and indicative of a warning rather than a fait accompli, but then a lovers' spat averted is possibly a smaller thing than a political turnabout. At least a crow's caw takes less energy to arrange than a flaming crack-up; only the timing of its caw makes it in any way out of the ordinary. And the energy contained in a situation is the key to the production of any ominous displays of that situation's dynamics.

On a less energetic level are meaningful "accidents." Perhaps instead of hearing a crow caw as one mentally berates one's sweetie, one will cut one's finger along with the carrot. The dy-

---

[9] It might be tempting for those living in 2005 (when I am adding this note for *Taking Power*) to read the events of the past few years into this omen—for instance the attack on the World Trade Center and the current neo-conservative dominance of the United States Government—but I believe this would be pushing it too far. Omens and divinations in general have a limited shelf-life. They display the ongoing currents of psychic energy, and to the extent that these currents determine the future, the omens seem to display the future. But currents of psychic energy can change from month to month, or even from hour to hour, and to expect them to hold good for nine years or more is to expect too much. Only in the case of an omen that occurred to mark some specific beginning like the publication of a book or the founding of a city—a true in*augur*ation—could one expect that it would retain its relevance for the duration of the event. Thus when Romulus and Remus held a contest to see who would found the city on the seven hills, Romulus won by spawning an omen of twelve eagles in flight, as opposed to Remus' six. This portended a duration of 1200 years, and in fact the period from the traditional date of Rome's founding in 753 b.c.e. to the surrender of the imperial regalia to Constantinople in 476 c.e. was 1229 years. But omens that just pop up in the middle of things should be interpreted as a diagnosis of the events in play at the time, and once that play is over the omen will lose its relevance.

namic is the same, but the mechanism is contained within the subject's personality, and so no occult or paranormal interaction need be hypothesized.

So we have a spectrum that ranges from public portents to the personal and strictly private, and this spectrum can be nicely interpreted as one that ranges from great energy to trifling. Political sea changes create lots of ecstasy and anguish, and the anticipation generated before the event by the hundreds of thousands of people who will be directly affected by it should be sufficient to spawn some impressive synchronicities. But when I'm thinking mean thoughts about my sweetie, that's just me, and so the coincidence will be a small one. And if I'm not paying attention, I'll miss it.

When we look at omens as being produced by the psychic energy within a situation, the similarity of their dynamic to that of conjuring becomes clear. Omens occur when a situation has a power overload that manifests as an event analogous to the way the energy is moving in that situation. This overload usually occurs because the situation contains more significance than the people involved in it will acknowledge—not to other people nor even to themselves—and so the tension is kept from release as conscious thought and must instead discharge as an objective display. With conjuring, on the other hand, we use artificial means to overload the situation with power in hopes that it will discharge as an event that will help us get what we want. It's the same dynamic, except that omens are its natural occurrence and conjurations are its technical exploitation.

Finally, we should consider the subject of omens in conjuring. Briefly, they don't mix well. If you're conjuring and you get any omen more impressive than a flight of birds or a break in the clouds, then that is energy wasted on display, energy that should be working to manifest the result you desire. Nor should you divine after conjuring to see how well it went, since the energy that goes to work the oracle would also be wasted. The best omen that a conjuration can produce is a result that accomplishes your will.

But this is not to say that you should ignore or repress the appearance of a decisive omen if such should appear; it may be telling you to change your procedure, your strategy, or your view of the situation you want to affect. As an example, I can recall a time when a friend of mine set up a ritual designed to destroy the negative thought and habit patterns within the participants' personalities. We were each given a dark and a light piece of cake. We then entered a period of individual gnosis wherein we identified the dark pieces with the negative aspects of personality, and the light pieces with the positive. Finally we ate the light pieces and put the dark ones into an ornate silverplate bowl where they were to be destroyed.

The fuel for destruction was a quantity of pure grain alcohol. Curiously, however, almost as soon as the cakes were set alight, the bowl began to melt, dripping hot metal all over my friend's nicely finished table. The fire was hastily smothered, the ritual aborted. The dark cakes, incidentally, were scarcely even warm. (A good wick does not burn.)

The omen was obvious to everyone except the host, though he had to admit the sense of it once it was explained. This is simply that negative personality patterns can never be destroyed; if we try, we'll destroy their container—our total selves—before the negativity is even touched. Further research has convinced me that the energy these negative patterns generate can be transformed into positive powers without changing the habit itself at all. The trick is simply to be aware of our pathologies as pathologies (and not as justified responses to an awful world), and then synthesize spirits whose sole function is to shift the energy from its negative application into something we can use. Thus may our pathologies be made profitable, each another engine to augment the momentum of our wills.

This essay was written in December of 1994.

# Spare's Ontology

The whole question of "What is real?" is one that has plagued the pursuit of knowledge ever since people became sufficiently aware of themselves to realize it needed an answer. A major difficulty is the problem of what is objective and what is subjective, or what is really out there and what is just projected out onto it by our own biases—our hopes, needs, fears and preconceptions, conscious and unconscious, admitted and denied. All we can know is what we perceive, so it is impossible to be perfectly objective, and yet objective reality is real enough, as anyone knows who has been in an automobile accident. The elimination of the perceiver's bias is one major aim of the scientific method, with its emphasis on measurement and replication intending to ensure that scientific theories work for anyone competent to apply them. But these safeguards reach their limit as soon as we begin to study anything that may be conscious, for mind may not be measured and will show a perverse defiance to attempts to fit it into repeatable experiments. Even so, certain academic psychologists still work to reduce all mental functions to what may be quantified in a laboratory setting, and come to the wholly logical conclusion that mind is no more than a side effect of the existence of nervous tissue. This makes as much sense as trying to set a broken leg with prayer and is the clearest possible proof that strict scientific methodology breaks down at this point.

Magick attempts to provide a middle ground between science and credulity, but this does not mean we escape the objective/subjective conundrum. Instead we rephrase the problem as that of macrocosm and microcosm. In magickal usage the macrocosm consists of the powers in the universe beyond us. The microcosm consists of the powers we have inside us. Traditionally, magicians have presumed that one or another of the ancient planetary mythologies can provide a symbolism descriptive of the powers available to us. The powers are personified as "the gods" who somehow project their particular powers in from the outside, and the human entity—as the "creation" or "emanation" of these gods—is a composite of these powers, which we thus experience from the inside. Once the magician chooses such a symbolic architecture, he or she has available the techniques of ceremonial magick to manipulate the powers this architecture includes, and through these techniques can either exalt a power or abase it, either draw on it or diminish it as his or her will might determine.

Thus does the magician acquire a symbolic interface through which he or she might manipulate power, and this without being obliged to deal with the question of what power *as such* really *is*.

The key to the effective use of any symbolic system is the complete unconscious assimilation of its components by the magician who uses it. In the Golden Dawn tradition this is done by memorization of the symbolism, ceremonial initiation in terms of the symbolism, and, most importantly, astral discipline. That is, one must be willing to impose the Rosicrucian structure onto one's astral visions, to require that whatever displays they choose to make be in terms of the imagery used by that system . Aleister Crowley, for one, is quite clear about this, insisting that we banish as demonic deceivers any entities who resist the requirement that they so conform. In my own personal experience this was hardly necessary, for my visions seemed anxious to do so. This was hardly reassuring to me, making it obvious that my unconscious was willing to take on *any* imagery, so long as it was self-consistent and able to include all the more conspicuous dualities that entertain our existence. This the Golden Dawn system surely does, and admirably so. Nonetheless, I found the whole notion of self-programming of symbolism to be personally repugnant. Thus as soon as it was clear to me that this was, in fact, the purpose of Rosicrucian training, I wanted no more part of it. My teacher at the time, Frater O.T.L., hearing my loud and articulate denunciation of the Rosicrucian option, graciously recommended that I look into the writings of an English sorcerer named Austin Osman Spare. The essence of Spare's magick lies in his solution to the objective/subjective, macrocosm/microcosm conundrum that we just covered. Spare addressed the problem with a direct attack, coming up with what can only be described as a practical solipsism—solipsism being the belief that the self is the only object of knowledge and thus, by extension, the only thing that exists. "What is there to believe, but in Self?" he asks in *The Book of Pleasure.* "And Self is the negation of completeness as reality. No man has seen self at any time. We are what we believe and what it implies by a process of time in the conception; creation is caused by this bondage to formula." (p. 1) Which is to say, what we believe determines what we experience, which determines what we are, which, over time, determines what is, because through our presumptions we shape whatever comes into contact with us, according to our power. Reality is the objective residue of a subjective process. In his *Focus of Life*, Spare elaborates:

> Eternal, without beginning is Self; without end am I; there is no other power or substance. The everchanging modifications and diversities we see are the results of forgetfulness, misinterpreted as nightmare senses. When the Self again desires, then *I* only and nothing else shall remain. Permitting all things, whatsoever is imagined comes out of it. (p. 21)

To give an idea of the dynamic in all this, in *The Book of Pleasure* Spare offers the argument of me (the reader) and a butterfly. I am conscious of being "I," the butterfly is conscious of being "I," and therefore my consciousness and that of the butterfly are the same. Spare errs in presenting this as a logical syllogism, in which terms it must fail, but it isn't really logic he's giving. Instead it's a description of the facts of his perception, upon which he based his magick, which worked.

The consequences of accepting that my "I" (me!) is the same as your "I" and the same as every other self-aware "I" in the whole of existence—that it's all at bottom a common experience made separate only by our belief in our alienation—are somewhat far-reaching. The Golden Rule becomes a truism and the decision to eat flesh presupposes a willingness eventually to be eaten. But to think that I am fundamentally the same as that bitch mosquito I just swatted, or that sonofabitch who cut me off on the Turnpike this afternoon, well, it's just too difficult to believe and so we don't, mostly. Creation is the result of this separation, the result of all the points of view—identical in source, essence and being both with each other and with the primordial I—seeing Self as something to eat, to fuck, or to flee from so as to keep from being eaten. From, again, *The Focus of Life*:

> And in this living nightmare, where *all* is cannibalism. Why dost thou deny thyself? Verily, Man resembles his creator, in that he consumes himself in much filth.
>
> Heaven gives indiscriminately of its superabundance to make the ghastly struggle called existence.
>
> The necessity was a deliberate serving of its own pleasure—becoming more alien. Remoteness from self is pain and precocious creation. (p. 7)

The necessity of creation was a deliberate serving of pleasure to the I, letting it see Self as a ground to be mined for pleasure, an object, not really Self at all. With this split came pain, and a desire to avoid pain even as pleasure was more fervently pursued. The split spawned millions of species and thousands of stratagems from fins to hard shells, from flight to pheromones, all the efflorescent life of the natural world. And in essence the split is simply belief embodied in flesh, the biological reification of "a process of time in the conception." To the extent we can recognize and reintegrate these, if only through an erasure of our own belief, the Cosmic Momentum behind Infinite Creation will be ours to tap, to do our wills.

At least that's the way Spare had it, which certainly does not mean that's the way things really are, even though his magick was effective. We can just as easily say that his self-alienated solipsism is simply an effective attitude to have when addressing power to do magick, even if existence in itself is not solipsistic. After all, the only way we can encounter the powers of magick is through our perception; we can even say that everything in consciousness is either a source of power for manipulation or else something that inhibits our manipulation of it. The fact is that what is *really* out there is not that important magickally. What matters is the way we take it in, the underlying assumptions we have over what it is, and what we are able to do with it. Optimism and pessimism are obvious examples of such assumptions, attitudes that can color our whole approach to life. More subtle are our preconceptions concerning what is possible, on what is and isn't connected in the "outside" world. Through taking the solipsistic attitude that All is Self, Spare evades the problem by making everything "inside," and All Things have their connections there.

So for Spare it is our habitual attitudes that hold us back, our *beliefs* as opposed to our *ideas*.[10] It is as if our beliefs are tracks that run parallel to power, drawing on it to move us along but without allowing us to address it directly, to tap it deliberately and exploit it. We must leave these tracks if we would do so.

For Spare, belief is the main obstacle to the work of the magician, with beliefs concerning the nature of spirit and psyche the most insidious of all. "Religions are the projections of incapacity," he writes in *The Book of Pleasure*, "the imaginations of fear, the veneer of superstition…while oftimes the ornament of imbecility… What you have ordained in your righteousness is your very rack, imagined though it be!" (p. 1) Faith he condemns as mere self-delusion, since it "'protects' but does not change the vital." For instance, if a man has faith that some benevolent deity has saved him from his personal pack of demons and that he is thus no longer

---

10 The English Chaos magician Peter J. Carroll proposes the intriguing notion that the difference between a belief and an idea is that an idea may be true, while a belief is always false. Ideas may be true because they are merely recognitions of patterns in what is perceived. Beliefs are always false because they define the way things are in an absolute sense, and the Absolute is something that does not permit any manner of definition.

their puppet (in spite of usually ample evidence to the contrary), then he will believe that there is nothing more to be done and will not take the trouble to meet them on their own ground and bind them into submission, which is the only way to control them with any degree of reliability.

"When faith perishes, the 'Self' shall come into its own… Myself, I have not seen a man who is not God already."

But then even beliefs that define man as a god do not escape Spare's condemnation, for he is equally derisive of traditional magick. "Others praise ceremonial Magic, and are supposed to suffer much Ecstasy! Our asylums are crowded, the stage is over-run! Is it by symbolizing that we become the symbolized? Were I to crown myself King, should I be King? Rather should I be the object of disgust or pity." (p. 2) He tells us that magick is a natural thing, our ability to spawn events as if by chance, ceremony more a style of living than any sort of production. And he dismisses the traditional practice of classifying different types of power according to their places in a theosophical scheme. "The freedom of energy is not obtained by its bondage, great power not by disintegration. Is it not because our energy (or mind stuff) is already bound over and divided, that we are not capable, let alone magical?" (p. 3)

The unbinding of mind-stuff is the essence of Spare's approach to magick—that and also its channeling in ways that do not bind it, that allow it to be focused according to will without putting any restrictions on the magician's ability to specify its use.

For Spare, it isn't just beliefs concerning the nature of the divine architecture that bind our power, but any belief short of Self-love. Self-love is an acceptance of and ecstasy in the Self as a whole, the sum of all possibilities in all times and places, what he calls Kia. Without definition, its name a designation rather than a description, Kia is a typical mystic Absolute and can be equated with the Chinese Tao, the Qabalistic Ain Soph, and the Neoplatonic One. "Obvious but unintelligible, without form, its design most excellent… How mighty it is, in its assertion of *'Need not be—Does not matter'*! Self-love in complete perspective, serves its own invincible purpose of ecstasy. Supreme bliss simulating opposition is its balance... Could we but imitate its law, all creation without command would unite to serve our purpose in pleasure and harmony." (p. 8) Which is to say, our cosmic purpose as nodes of perception in Kia is to enjoy it, taking all seeming contradiction and conflict as variations on its infinite power—power which, once we recognize it for what it is, will be ours to use. But we cannot so long as we are enthralled by beliefs smaller than love for Kia, for these inevitably trap us in the snare of duality—simulated opposition, to be sure, but deadly enough for those who are caught in it. It is out of our conceptions that duality comes, out of our tendency to make distinctions.

Whenever we make a distinction—whenever we say "It is *this* and not *that*"—we are unconsciously affirming that *that* is equally real to *this*, and thus must in time supplant it. If I believe *order* exists, then so also must *disorder*. If disorder did not exist then order would be a constant state and would never assert itself enough to be believed in. If I[11] say *male* exists, then so also must *female*; if there were only asexual reproduction, then there would be no way to make the distinction, and only *life* would be recognized, whose opposite would be *death*. And so it is with any distinction we allow ourselves to make. "Duality in some form or another is consciousness of existence. It is the illusion of time, size, entity, etc.—the world's limit. The dual principle is the quintessence of all experience, no ramification has enlarged its early simplicity, but is only its repetition, modification or complexity, never is its evolution complete." (p. 9)

Now for distinctions like predator and prey, male and female, and life and death, the dual principle is obvious and easy enough to accept, at least in the abstract. Nor, on this level, is it anything we can easily render down for the power in it, these distinctions being the result of the collective machination of Self and I—the pattern

---

[11] Or, more properly, if some bisexual worm living in the primordial ooze decides male exists, then so also must female. The sexual distinction was established back close to the beginning, one so fundamental it is written into our very cells, and may be 'transcended' only with great fortitude and determination.

of Creation itself. So if we are to tap the power of Kia behind duality, the dualities have to be closer to home. A good place to start looking is among those distinctions at the root of our emotional reactions—energetic responses whose power will be available to accomplish our wills, if only we can reconcile the distinctions.

The distinctions that we enforce, that we insist are truth, are the ones that constitute the crippling beliefs. Suppose, for instance, that a farmer looks at his field and tells himself that it is lush. If he has accepted the dual principle, he will simultaneously affirm that there is also land that is arid, and that in time his field may become arid, too. But if his self-interest requires that his land *will be* lush, and the rainfall diminishes, then his belief in lushness will cause him to irrigate. For a time, perhaps even for several lifetimes, this tactic will succeed, but ultimately the salts in the water will build up in the soil, making it not only arid but a stinking desert, sterile to all life. His enforcement of his belief makes the poles of the duality more extreme, bringing on the violent intervention of the opposite—crippling to Self-love and the power that comes out of it. As Spare writes in his *Anathema of Zos*: "Belief foreshadows its inversion. Overrun with forgotten desires and struggling truths, ye are their victim in the dying and begetting law." (p. 13)

The way of no belief would simply be to change crops to account for the shifting rainfall, going from corn to grain to grass as required, always taking care not to strain the soil for the sake of short-term profit. This requires sensitivity and thought, a mind brimming with ideas, but not belief, which only stifles the creativity needed to be in harmony with what is perceived, to truly love Self.

Of course scientific technologies can be applied to situations like this to extend the reign of one element of a duality over its opposite. To cut down on salt build-up, drains may be installed in a field to carry off waste water. But the reversal will still come eventually and will be that much more extreme—for instance salty soil littered with clay tiles instead of just salty soil. Any technology that does not account for all elements of its component dualities

will ultimately fail. The whole perspective of scientific material-
ism, by treating all things as dead and devoid of spirit, will also.

But while the dual principle is a subtle problem in physical
technology, in moral and social technology it is overtly malignant.
The most blatant example of a moral duality is that of good and
evil. To exalt what is perceived as "good" or, worse, to try to wipe
out "evil," only strengthens what we don't want, causing it to
manifest in ever purer forms. The Catholic Church's desire to wipe
out the perceived evil of disunion and heresy caused it to create its
Inquisition, which itself became an unsurpassed instrument of
horror. America's attempt to banish the evil of Communism cul-
minated in the abscess of the Vietnam War. And then when it
lightened up and just pushed the equilibrium in an abstract military
sense, Communism collapsed under the weight of its own dogma.

The good/evil duality plays havoc with our inner states of mind
as well as the course of history. If we allow the situations or people
we encounter to in any way offend us, Self-love and the power it
supplies will be impossible to maintain. To believe that something
is offensive and combat it, even if only in our minds, is to split it
off from Self and lose our power to perceive it accurately and
manipulate it decisively. Also, the energy we devote to opposing it
will give it a sharper definition and a greater strength.

Of course it isn't just anger and offense that can alienate us
from Kia. Fear does it, too, as does guilt, sentimentality, greed and
pride. In Spare's published work he implies that the source of these
is our limited beliefs. For myself, I must say that I don't think he
goes deeply enough. In my own experience, beliefs that have a
foundation in an emotional response to circumstances are generally
products of biases that are wired into personality, psychic reflexes
that may be interpreted as independent spirits or demons and managed through an ongoing program of evocation and magickal control. Spare, on the other hand, treated the problem as one of beliefs
as such, and attempted to dismember them through two more general techniques—an exercise he called "the death posture" and the
use of a logical tool he called "the Neither-Neither principle." The
death posture is just that—a posture—so it isn't really relevant to

this essay, but the Neither-Neither fits right in, it being the corollary of the dual principle—its precise counterpart, in fact.

The point of the Neither-Neither is that just as the assertion of any distinction makes necessary its opposite, so the combination in mind of a distinction and its opposite will nullify the duality and release the energy of the original assertion as an undifferentiated power that should then be used in magick. This energy Spare called "free belief."

The Neither-Neither works against any belief, from a belief in the existence of any "permanent" object (just imagine it over time) to emotional necessities to the airiest philosophies. Of course the more committed one is to a belief, the more difficult it will be to conjure up the necessary opposite; in cases where the belief seems absolutely necessary, it will take great personal power just to see the other half of the duality, and even more to transcend the two halves to leap to the level where both may be held in mind simultaneously. Also, just because a person is able to accept both halves intellectually doesn't mean that he or she must accept them both as equally valid courses of action. That is, it is important to distinguish matters of Fact from matters of Will. To apply the Neither-Neither to the statement "I am alive" is to affirm that "I will die," but this does not mean I am thus obliged to make it so. So long as it is my will, I may fervently promote the Life half of the duality. But my purpose will be supported if I can accept the reality of the Death half, for by dancing close to it great power may be snatched, power that may be used to live all the more triumphantly.

To close, I would only remark that once you generate free belief, you should always focus it into some sort of magickal working, for if you leave it lying around it will energize one or another of your dominant demons, bringing the alienation back all over again, even if in a different form.

The first version of this essay was published as "Spares Ontologie" (German translation by "Ikkah Zod-ka") in *Thanateros* no. 1,

Vienna, 1990. The first English publication was in *Nuit-Isis* no. 10, Oxford, 1992.

# On the Virtuous Wizard

## An Analysis of Ethics in the Occult

*"For what shall it profit a man, if he gain the whole world, and lose his soul?" (Mark 8:36)*

## I. What Ethics Here Must Be

Ethics have always had a somewhat alien place in magick. Customarily the standards for righteous living have been set by the State and the established Church, two institutions that have consistently worked to push all things sorcerous into the deepest pit of Hell. On the other hand, if we allow for the convention that true morality comes from God, and the magician seeks to insinuate self into that high position, then magicians make their own morality.

Even so, certain standards of behavior do seem to impose themselves. As we work to create our own universes, shouldn't we regard duration as a criterion for success? Don't we do better to conjure up pleasant circumstances that generate their own support than strained circumstances that must feed upon outside sources until all shrivel in alienated starvation? Shouldn't happiness and prosperity result from our efforts, rather than pain, foreboding and bitter regret?

So we have two essentially separate subjects to deal with. On the one hand we must dispose of all the "ethical" considerations imposed by State and Church that have nothing to do with either magickal prowess or our relations with our fellow humans and the natural world. On the other hand, we must look very closely at the power flows the various types of magickal operation set up, our abilities to endure them over the long run, and their capacity for enhancing our lives rather than wearing us down or locking us into minimal destinies. Simply by examining the "energy budget" of an operation over time, we can obtain an objective criterion for assigning an ethical status to it.

Curiously, however, once we begin to examine which power flows help us, and which corrupt, thwart and destroy, we may come to conclusions similar to those reached by some of the great teachers of those same established religions that have bedeviled us for so long. Not that I thus bow to the authority of Yahweh, but then perhaps those great teachers didn't either. We can easily speculate that ancient mages like Moses and Jesus recognized the same power dynamics that we do, but offered their conclusions as the commandments of the Lord God Almighty just to get them some respect.

So I hold our situation to be this: we can do right and wrong in magick, but our acts do not concern the Creator of the Universe. Rather, the reward and punishment come as consequences of the power flows our conjurations set up. The laws of sorcery have little to do with morality, but instead act as the psychic equivalent of the laws of physics. Our only punishment is failure, and the damage caused by the failure process. Thus when we violate psychic laws, psychic destruction results. Just as you may crash your new Lexus through injudicious acceleration, so can you wreck your life through injudicious conjuration. The experience of the two circumstances is similar: the deed is done, cannot be undone, and the whole thing is a mess. It may also hurt. In any case the consequences will be obvious at once, even if they take a lifetime to unfold.

By associating magickal ethics with psychic cause and effect, we liberate them from orthodox dogmas of good and evil. We can raise and focus power, and we can do it with grace, or else with corruption and commotion. This more than any "standard of behavior" determines morality in magick. And this approach is appropriate to the plane whereupon we work magick, where we use belief as a tool for manipulating reality instead of as a mental representation of what is and is not "real." Orthodox theological architectures of good and evil are fabrications of belief maintained by believers who animate these architecture's reality through their fear and devotion. Patterns of magickal consequence, on the other hand, derive directly from the way the animation itself operates. What this animation achieves determines the beneficence of the result, and we direct the animation with will, not intellect.

## II. Avenues for Error

Though we can easily call self-destructive occult working "black magick," the term doesn't help much as an analytical tool. It mostly just implies magick the speaker doesn't approve of. Now I readily admit that there are types of magick that *I* don't approve of, as I shall make clear in the pages to come. But calling these sorts of magick "black" only expresses my opinion, and misses the fact that very specific dynamics of energy flow distinguish them and argue against their use. It seems better to develop a terminology that articulates these facts than to base our thinking on superficial dualities like white and black.

We might more usefully divide up the problem by simply recognizing two avenues for botching the work: how we raise energy and what we do with it once we have it. Our approach can then transcend symbolical systems and specific techniques for raising power. Prayer and fasting, on the one hand, and sexual intercourse augmented by psychedelic drugs, on the other, both seem like methods for raising energy that can have a place in modern magick, depending upon both the temperaments of the operators and the specific operations they perform. To say that one is holy and the other blasphemous, or one white and the other black, only allows ignorance, fear and spiritual arrogance to keep us from working as we must. Nonetheless, two methods of raising power do strike me as intrinsically malign and self destructive: vampirism and pacts with spirits. But you can easily avoid these if you have any self-control at all, and this avoidance does not require the exercise of any subtle judgment. You just have to know them as fatal mistakes that offer no recourse.

But when we begin to use the energy, then all the delicacies arise—the questions of energy imbalance, of pushing aside processes of natural development, of calling up entities that cannot be put down. By using energy we may acquire momentums that carry us all unwilling into disaster. By using energy we risk creating ideal worlds that turn into cages whose only door out opens into Death.

In any event both these realms of action—getting the energy ready and then applying it—involve fundamental activities of sorcery and so deserve coverage in any essay concerning itself with sorcerous ethics. This will be our task in the next three sections. But unfortunately I must first note the existence of activity that has no connection at all to magick, but nonetheless haunts it at the fringes. I refer to the acts of criminals who attempt to use magick as some sort of philosophical or existential justification for behaviors that can have none.

Just because a person calls it sex magick when he sodomizes an eight-year-old, and does it on an altar within a circle, that doesn't make it any less a felony. If a magickal operation results in a victim with a complaint under the criminal code, and there exists physical evidence to support that complaint, then the civil authorities have evidence of a crime and the civil authorities should prosecute it. This in particular applies to fraud, assault, rape and murder. If a reasonably intelligent police detective can understand the essentials of what happened, then it isn't magick no matter how mysterious the façade. It's just crime.

Magickal justifications for such behavior range from the simply predatory to the most heartfelt rationalizations. The pedophiles seem the most sincere, but no magickal justification exists for rites involving the sexual participation of children. Growing in a presexual state with unformed chakras and a sleeping Kundalini, children can contribute no energy to amplify or enhance a ritual, no hormonal forces to push the participants into new states of power. Traditionally in magick, the only role they've ever had in ritual was as skryers—for instance gazing into a puddle of ink to glimpse the spirit the wizard had invoked, and hear its message. The rationale was that the child's innocence would enable the child to perceive the entity without admixture from the child's own unconscious. But no traditional magick, however heretical, has found its power in corrupting that innocence. Until they pass into pubescence, children have nothing to contribute to a sexual ritual except their presence as a screen upon which the pedophile can project his or her own twisted meanings. The protection of children under such circumstances is the business of their parents, and of the police.

## III. Raising Energy

The magician has three sources of energy from which he or she can take power to work magick: his or her own self, other people, and the natural world. Of these, we must consider "other people" as the most ethically questionable, but only in certain specific circumstances. We will get to these in due course.

The magician should approach his or her own self as the most important energy source he or she will ever have to deal with. Simply by being alive we produce tremendous amounts of psychic energy, and if we have the presence of mind and technique to transform and store it instead of dissipating and wasting it, we will have the perfect tool to grasp all the power we need.

We can acquire power from self through mastery of personality, through sexual discipline, and through our intrinsic connections to the Absolute. We may directly address this link to the Absolute by means of manipulation of our subtle bodies—the Kundalini Serpent and its companion power flows which together tie spirit to flesh to make for conscious life. In addition, we may use psychoactive drugs to augment and enhance emotion, sexuality and powerflow. Of these factors, the ones with ethical relevance are emotions, sex and drugs, though mastery of the subtle body can help one practice vampirism, which we will cover a few pages hence.

The wizard must master the components of personality simply to survive the process of empowerment. As Carlos Castaneda's don Juan points out, a cracked gourd may look perfectly sound, but when you fill it with food it will split and spill your sustenance in the dirt. Thus we must discover and repair personality flaws before we win any great power, lest our sorcery push us apart from within and we end up dead, in prison, in the asylum, or living in a pup tent hidden in a ravine.

The solution to this problem of repair mostly involves the integrity of one's Word, the strength of one's will, mental control, control of the subtle body, and management of emotions. We must possess an uncompromised Word before we begin any magickal work, and we can obtain it through the essential exercise of keeping it. After all, how can you expect the great spirit Brazelsnatz to respect your Word if it doesn't even have the power to cause you to take your child to the zoo when you said you would? As for strength of will, I find ascetic exercises like Aleister Crowley's *Liber III vel Jugorem* to have great value. And we may obtain mental control and control of the subtle body through exercises of raja yoga and those that involve manipulation of the Kundalini, chakras and such like. I have covered both these in my other writings—the raja yoga in *Stealing the Fire from Heaven*, the subtle body work in my essay "The Subtle Body."

Once we have obtained some competence in these, we should have an awareness of which psychic sore spots tend to most trouble our exercises, simply because we cannot shut them up. And we will see clearly that we must shut them up before we can accomplish any serious magickal work.

Psychic sore spots manifest most forcefully as emotional rants that continue until they exhaust themselves, rants that return again and again and follow the same essential theme each time. Until we recognize them as pathological, we will simply interpret them as justified denunciations of an imperfect world. Once we see them as flaws, however, we can use sorcerous techniques to both interrupt the rants and reroute the energy that animates them so it promotes our purposes. For instance, we can synthesize spirits specifically dedicated to transforming the energy from the negative emotion into some positive power, any thing from specific abilities like literary creativity or sexual charisma to more generalized powers like overall magickal effectiveness. Since we make no attempt to repress the energy, we run no risk of pathology, and if we have manufactured the spirit properly[12], the rant should vanish immediately upon calling for its help.

Now obviously this sort of magick has no negative ethical ramifications. In fact it is inherently positive since it can preclude any rash action inspired by a lack of emotional control. And together with exercises of yoga and subtle body manipulation, it helps to prepare self to handle the more vigorous power flows produced by magickal operations involving the sex act and the use of psychoactive drugs.

Assuming the sex act is either autoerotic or between consenting adults, and the drugs are either cultivated by the magician or purchased with money obtained through legitimate means, I do not see that these have any ethical component either. But some people might disagree with me, so I should make my reasoning explicit.

The most obvious and also specious objection to sex magick is made by theists who believe the Creator of the Universe designed the sex act exclusively for procreation and that to exploit it for magickal purposes somehow offends this Supreme Being. I reply that the Creator of the Universe eats galaxies for breakfast and so could hardly care what we here on this cosmic speck do with our genitals. God may have active awareness of the fall of a sparrow, because by its death God loses an eye. That, however, does not mean that God cares. When a consciousness has $10^{23}$ eyes, the loss of one makes no difference. But the consciousness still does notice.

So I counter theism with a hedonistic pantheism, a faith for which sex magick appears a most natural sacrament. As Aleister Crowley's Great Revelation tells us, existence is "divided for

---

[12] Ideally with the help of your Holy Guardian Angel.

love's sake, for the chance of union." Wizards, however, will notice another ethical concern relevant to the sex act. Simply put, the sex act manufactures sacred elixirs brimming with creative power, and we must treat them as potent fluids capable of creating worlds. Thus we must not profane the Sacrament by treating these as so much piss and snot that we wipe up and throw away as soon as we've had our fun. With regard to this concern I would simply emphasize: *Do not profane the sacrament!* Once you begin this type of working, commit yourself to continue it for the rest of your life. Treat sexual fluids as vehicles for vital force. Whenever you have them available, either consume them as a Eucharist, use them to charge a talisman, or, if they be spilled or otherwise made unusable, at least banish them.

The matter of drugs doesn't pertain to magickal ethics at all, except to the extent that they impair the user's survival or the performance of tasks magickal or mundane. And the individual has the right to judge this for himself, assuming his or her behavior does not cause such disruption that it imposes itself on the neighbors. But then any competent magician should have the ability to keep a lid on that. Beyond that, the State has responsibility for what it chooses to suppress, and it must justify this suppression with its own logic. And whatever that logic happens to be, it has nothing to do with any ethics at all. (On the other hand, I would regard the involuntary "dosing" of unsuspecting individuals as a species of assault, one of the crimes mentioned at the end of the last section.)

Even so, the magickal ethicist has to wonder if the objection to drugs in magick, and to sex magick also, might have root in the fact that they work as well as they do. Psychoactive drugs, especially cannabis and the psychedelics, produce a feedback loop that can promote the work of anyone with a modicum of self-control and a willingness to risk using them. Both can make it easier to visualize the power flows during subtle body exercises, and the psychedelics tend to excite these flows, making them all the more palpable. Being more vivid and palpable, we may more easily manipulate and control them, and cause them to act with greater effect. At the same time, well-controlled, effective power flows make the management of the drug experience a matter of straight-forward sorcerous technique. Simply banishing and defining one's chakras and Kundalini can do much to stop a panic response to LSD. Such control gives these drugs a certain usefulness for conjuring—sexual or otherwise—when a few hours of amplified consciousness can bring changes well worth the next day's lethargy. Also, cannabis in small doses does much to make the astral experience more explicit. Psychedelics, on the other hand, make the experience of the physical body far too persistent to allow for the step out of it that distinguishes astral consciousness.

So with sex and drugs the magician's conjuring gains the potential for acquiring some real punch, becoming quite capable of generating the peculiar realities the competent practitioner requires. And since sorcerers tend to prefer realities free of the interference by corporations and the civil state, these institutions do what they can to inhibit our work. They fear that once we come into our power, we might direct our opposition from an ontological level against which they have no defense—they having no psyches to counter what would essentially be a psychic attack. Thus they seek to hide the sex act behind thickets of custom, religion and commerce; thus they seek to ban all non-toxic agents of consciousness expansion. But, again, this has nothing to do with ethics, only with the primal struggle between a sclerotic civilization and a culture coming to birth. We would do well to pay close attention to the evolution of this contest as the new century unfolds.

With the prohibitions against drugs and sex thus put aside as civil and sacerdotal taboo, we move on to possibilities for obtaining power from other people, an option far more open to ethical question. The morality of using other people as power sources depends on one's relationship with the people involved. Five distinct contexts for taking power present us with five distinct moral dynamics, only one of which stands out as really evil. The human power sources in these five categories are: 1) magickal colleagues,

2) adoring fans, 3) devotees, 4) opponents in magickal combat, and 5) the victims of vampires.

1) By magickal colleagues I mean those people with whom we work to raise energy, and with whom we share the results. So long we give the energy as freely as we take it, we engage in a psychic partnership, something not at all open to ethical criticism. Varieties of such partnership range from lovers in an act of sex magick to a lodge working of the Ordo Supremo Mystica. The dynamic will be similar for all: a mutual raising of energy in conjuration, followed by each individual taking his or her share and absorbing it, or else all devoting it to a mutually desired result.

2) Adoring fans want you to have their energy, and you would be rude to refuse to accept it. Whether they adore you as a rock & roll star, a football hero, a war president, or the lead in the high school play, with their ovation the present a gift of power, so have the grace to absorb it efficiently. Smile, wave, and wheel it into your belly chakra for storage, but never consider that all that enthusiasm has anything *at all* to do with your worth as a person. Your performance or the events you represent conjures an automatic release of power from the ecstatic crowd—a catharsis. As its focal point, you'll do better to absorb it deliberately than to let it have a free hand on your aura, with potentially obsessive results.

3) The relationship of devotee to guru is ideally one of reciprocal exchange—the devotee directing devotion to the guru, the guru using that power to give magickal assistance, healing energy, and bliss in return. So long as the devotee is satisfied with the subservient role, and realizes that he or she will never have any other, I see no ethical questions arising here either.

4) We may regard energy we take from opponents in magickal combat as booty of war. Your opponent puts his or her power at risk in order to hurt you with it, so if you can capture it, you can hardly be censured if you digest it for your own use. If you have but the teeth for it, you can consume whatever energy they have sent against you and whatever you may take through any link they have foolishly left between their projectile and themselves. But to digest it you will need a spirit that can transform the energy of

conflict hurled at you into something more neutral, lest the martial energy that you win inspire your own martial spirits to act rashly.

You also need to stop chewing and swallowing before you get to anything *intrinsic* about your opponent. Do not consume any part of the psychic center, but only whatever raw power you can worry out of it, this to prevent any admixture of their essence from tainting your own.

5) Vampirism festers as an enduring sore spot in questions of magickal ethics, since the practice is real, pathological, and contagious in a slow rot/decadent sort of way. Unlike the undead bloodsuckers of folklore and film, the living vampire steals energy as sexual excitement, avarice, political enthusiasm or religious devotion. Unfortunately, anyone can take up this practice whether they've had magickal training or not, though competence in the magickal manipulation of the subtle body certainly makes the theft more efficient and sure. But then what does the vampire actually steal, and how does it effect vampire and victim?

In both tradition and practice, either the victim must invite the vampire, or he or she must go to it. Thus the victim must at least technically acquiesce, though the invitation the victim offers need have no more substance than a not-quite-innocent curious look. And some people tend to conform to a particular victim "type"; they simply find it easy to take the vampire's bait. They experience the glamour the vampire displays as enormously seductive, the façade promising unspeakable adventures in virtue or vice, though the fundamental dynamic always tends toward a feeding. Such victims find that acquiescence to feeding brings them pleasure, this felt as orgasm, political fervor or religious surrender, depending on the vampire's mode of working. If the victim can find rest in the Sleep of Death that follows, he or she will surely come back for more, again and again, until there is nothing left worth mentioning.

The sin of vampirism is simply theft, a psychic con-job that corrupts the vampire even as it drains the victim. The energy consumed gave the victim his or her special momentum, so the vampire absorbs that momentum along with the energy—the victim's direction as well as the vital force that pushed the victim along it.

The life imperatives thus absorbed will be subtle. The vampire will experience them as uncharacteristic reflexes that will start out merely troublesome but which may ultimately contradict imperatives the vampire needs for survival. More likely they will simply compromise the vampire's rigor. With repeated feedings the vampire will bloat with power, but without any real direction, and the taint of nothingness will infect everything of value that the vampire might have accumulated.

The vampire has two facades, two strategies to use to attract willing victims: the private and the public. The private vampire holds out prurient companionship intended to lead the victim to orgasm while the vampire has none, then takes care to absorb whatever energy the victim emits. The public vampire holds out exclusive salvation—religious or political—to the faithful ones who embrace True Belief and accept the vampire as the Anointed Leader. To an outsider the devotion seems ludicrous, but outsiders do not take part in the energy dynamic and thus do not understand the feedback loop of vital force/charisma that sustains the relationship.[13] But though it is sufficient to ensure the loyalty of the vampire's flock, it can only corrode his or her psychic coherence, and can offer little assistance against the inevitable defiance of the outside world. In the end both religious and the political vampires run up close to annihilation and often cross over into it, as the careers of Jim Jones, David Koresh and Adolph Hitler make so clear.

The conspicuous feature of vampirism, the most blatant warning sign for those the vampire may be stalking, is what the vampire does with the energy he or she accumulates. Vampires characteristically can use power only to get more of the same sort of power, albeit of ever-diminishing quality. Their directionless bloat absorbs momentum like some psychic black hole, and cannot supply the thrust that real creativity requires. The enterprise, whether it involves nations or just a small circle of friends, inevitably loses its

---

[13] Which we must distinguish from the far more equitable devotion/power loop between guru and chela.

character, and most of its allure. Toward the end, if a potential victim can peer through the thinnest of facades, he or she will know enough to turn and walk away. The bait turns rotten, able to attract only vermin.

This would be a good spot to inject a reply to a certain school of vaguely theistic opponents to magick, opponents whom one suspects might be Christian but who don't make the usual arrogant appeal to the First Commandment. They instead propose that the Totality of Magickal Power has a finite quantity, as if it were a pizza from which we should ideally each take one slice. And from this presumption they conclude that those who practice magick use their craft to get more than their fair share, thus depriving others of their due. Thus must our art be antisocial, and conducive to evil. And so we shouldn't do it.

To this I can only reply that they have a false conception of power. Magickal power has no limit, so we do not need to hoard it for ourselves, but only to recognize it and bring it into flesh so it may animate, replenish and inspire our lives. We accomplish this bringing-in process by defining psychic conduits, strengthening them, and straightening out the kinks within them so power can flow through without turbulence.

Thus power does not consist of one pizza that we fight over. Rather, it is infinite, and we bring it in through plumbing that we must install. And since we each of us must perform our own installations, we may keep this matter entirely to ourselves. At this fundamental level there can be no involvement of ethics at all. The ethics are only in the details of the application.

Our last source of power is the natural world. Woven upon geologies and ecologies both material and subtle, this elemental web can provide power to anyone with the will to learn how. I have discovered in its knots and tangles superb places to take power to augment my own, so long as I cultivate a rapport with whatever environments I so use. Under certain specific circumstances, we can tap into essentially infinite sources of energy, with what we take from them limited only by our abilities to absorb it. But to do this with grace we need an exquisite sympathy, lest we drain the ecology of the psychic stuff it needs for self-sustenance.

Paradoxically, by taking a landscape to such a point of stress, we can better perceive its energetical features, including any special sources of power. If it does contain a specific power spot, it can serve as a worthy spigot for direct feeding. If the sorcerer can take energy from such a spot, he or she may need to feed for only a few minutes at most. So the normal flow resumes almost at once and the landscape suffers no loss.

For example, I know of a patch of woods convenient to my home. It was one of the first places I addressed when I began using the technique of treating the spiritual essence of a place as an elemental. An area of virgin forest surrounded by development, it has a discrete identity that indicates it possesses a spirit of its own, so by undergoing a sort of waking astral vision of it, I used astral conventions to learn the elemental's name, bind it with a ritual charge, and gain access to its energy flow. And from the beginning I did my best to sympathize with how much it had to give. It felt the most vigorous in late spring and early summer, while in fall and early spring it seemed like I had to pull the power out of it, and it did not recover quickly. So I limited my taking to when it seemed like it had power to spare, which worked well enough for the first three or four years.

But with the fifth spring I noticed a certain sluggishness, a lack of intensity when I should have felt a vernal torrent. So I called up the elemental to astral appearance and it told me I was making it sick. Apparently my growing competence in manipulating energy enabled me to absorb enough to make the woods suffer from the lack. But the elemental volunteered that the woods had a discrete source of power, and led me right to it. I found the spot on a high point with a good view of the wood's prime geological attribute. By naming this spot and binding it, it was as if I fitted it with a faucet from which I could drink directly. And because I used it at most for a half hour each week, I did not deprive the woods as a whole of the slow diffusion of power that provided their spiritual sustenance. My taking power from them after they had digested it, on the other hand, had become a burden.

Sympathy for dynamics such as these seems to me the essential criterion for righteous behavior while engaged in the sorcery of *genii loci*. Of course this can become a problem only when the sorcerer actually takes the energy. The sorcerer need have no concern when he or she uses the elemental to gain knowledge, sympathy for a particular power, or magickal assistance for a conjuration, as when the operator supplies the energy then uses the elemental to deliver it to a level of consequence that he or she otherwise could not reach. Since the elemental serves only as a guide, catalyst or conduit, no real energy exchange takes place and so the dynamic as such has nothing of moral consequence about it.

## IV. Pacts with Spirits and Other Ritual Sloppiness

In discussing elementals just now I made explicit use of "the spirit model" of sorcerous interaction, though I mixed my analysis with aspects of "the energy model." Simply put, I treat both the *genius* of the landscape and that of the power spot that nourishes it as specific spirits with whose power I can connect through the use of standard astral conventions. And I can do this without regard for their actual energetic characteristics. That is, the woods have a personal presence of sorts, so it seems accurate enough to treat them as an astral "person," but the power spot seems more like a mechanism to be manipulated. Even so, I treat it as if it were a spirit anyway, and my interaction seems to work as well as it would if it actually were.

So the spirit model is only a model, and no sort of absolute truth, but to my mind it provides the most powerful tool for working magick, and its use defines "sorcery" in an operational sense.

You can easily adapt it to any occult circumstance, allowing you to address any powers that you can define as if they were distinct spirits, and it offers precise techniques for managing your interactions with them. But to use it we must take a correct ethical attitude, and avoid an incorrect one, and some of the possible errors approach the nature of mortal sin. These involve formal pacts with spirits, though we may indulge in compromises less deliberate that can do more or less the same sort of damage. I find it difficult to say here where technical laxity crosses over into ethical fault, so in this section I will cover the whole spectrum, which I hope will clarify the need for clean practice throughout.

The dangers of working in the spirit model resemble those attendant to labor management anywhere. We have to keep the workers in their place, doing their tasks as needed without the sort of familiarity that might cause them to think they can run the whole show. Otherwise we will lose control, and magickal impotence, or even insanity, becomes a likely outcome.

Thus the spirit model has no place for consensus management or any other implications of equality, but should work more along feudal lines. You must take your place as the lord and demand fealty of your vassals, the spirits. Though you should address them with civility, they must accept your word as absolute.

As with any efficient system of management, proper procedure will serve as your foremost means of control. This includes all the protective tools of conjuring: circles, banishing rituals, and words of power that can license a spirit to depart, separate you from energy you have sent out, or pull back extensions of power from your aura. These are tools as basic as a dogcatcher's net and van, and if you don't perfect them, you can expect to get bitten.

The most important procedure consists of the ritual binding of a spirit upon one's first encounter with it. Banishing rituals can become routine—like throwing a circuit breaker before rewiring an electrical switch—but we must perform bindings as deliberate acts of will, with full concentration on the words of the charge and their meaning. The charge I use when I meet a spirit for the first time comes from a Græco-Egyptian ritual translated into English by

Charles Wycliff Goodwin in 1852. The ritual was adapted by Aleister Crowley to serve as his "Preliminary Invocation" to the *Goetia* in 1903. Its charge to the spirit reads like this:

> Hear Me: and make all Spirits subject unto Me: so that every Spirit of the Firmament and of the Ether: upon the Earth and under the Earth: on dry Land and in the Water: of Whirling Air and of Rushing Fire: and every Spell and Scourge of God may be obedient unto Me.

When spoken to the spirit with full concentration and intent, you may find it physically difficult to utter these words, as if the motion of your jaw were doing the subjugating. The difficulty here varies with the nature of the spirit. It will take more effort to bind the demon who personifies a deep childhood trauma than to bind the elemental of an inland sea. Your "dominion" over the elemental merely gives you the ability to open and close access to its power. But by binding the demon you pull a broken-off piece of your psyche back so it fits in with the rest of you, bringing it under sensible control, and you must confront all the implications of the original break to restore it to its place in your psychic structure.

Once we thus put our spirits under nominal control, we have the ability to interact with them safely, but only if we have the sense to keep the upper hand. For instance, we must never invite them into ourselves, a major risk with "possessive" techniques of divination like the Ouija Board. The spirit has to occupy the operator for it to work the planchette, and if the operator is an inexperienced adolescent, he or she risks possession by the worst sort of psychic scum. A child will not know how to banish, will have an immature subtle body, and will have a tendency to obey the spirit simply because its messages are coherent. As Aleister Crowley noted in his essay "The Ouija Board—A Note," we would be surely upset if some stranger came into our office and started ordering around our employees, or entered our homes and began to plan a dinner party. And yet people who use a Ouija board give over their minds and hands to "any strange intelligence that may be wandering about." And they do so "without taking the slightest precaution." (p. 319)

Crowley goes on to suggest that the Ouija Board can help a ceremonial magician interview specific angels or deities invoked within a properly consecrated circle. But in this case a trained sorcerer provides temporary residence to a very pure power, instead of a child offering itself to random specters of nameless atrocity, the conglomerated shells of the not-yet-rotten dead.

The obvious mistake of giving authority to a spirit just because it displays an apparently coherent intelligence leads us to the somewhat more sophisticated error of assuming that just because a spirit has power in one realm, it has competence in all others as well. Just because the great spirit Brazelsnatz can predict the weather doesn't mean it can tell you who your friends are. Unfortunately, if a person operates under a theistic bias, errors of this sort become almost inevitable. If we assume that all power comes from God (the Creator of the Universe Who has a Plan for us), then we can easily conclude that every spirit that acts with power must have our best interests at heart. The episode of Rasputin provides an instance of this fallacy in modern history, an error directly responsible for the deaths of millions. Of course Rasputin was a man rather than a spirit, but he did have conspicuous and irrefutable power to stop the bleeding consequent to the Czarevitch's hemophilia. The Czarina thus had justification for concluding that Rasputin possessed a certain sort of Grace. But unfortunately she also assumed that any and all Grace must come from the God she worshipped, the same God who provided the Holy Justification for her husband's absolute power. And since she assumed that this God possesses omniscience as well as omnipotence, it somehow followed that Rasputin had the competence to determine high appointments in the Russian government and even the strategy to follow in the war against the Central Powers. The Czarina's husband, Saint Nicholas II, as stupid as his wife and as pliant as she was stubborn, allowed her monk to have his way and so did they make the Revolution inevitable.

Just because an entity displays power in one realm does not mean it has knowledge of or influence over any other. Do not make the mistake of asking the spirit that promotes your career for advice on love and marriage, or you may end up making a career out of marriage.

That said regarding occult blunders, we should move on to address those practices that we may regard as actually evil. Of course what stands out here is what gives this section its name: pacts with spirits. What makes these immoral is the question of intent: willingness to surrender self to a being of limited horizon in return for access to its preternatural power.

I must here distinguish a pact from a sacrifice. With a pact the magician agrees to engage in future behavior in return for present favor. With a sacrifice the magician makes a payment of energy right now—anything from a dance or chant to incense or blood or semen—to give a spirit energy to act in the way the magician requires. Thus with the sacrifice we make an honorable bargain while the pact leads us to whoredom and slavery. Possibly the best known pact in history was made by Abraham, son of Terah, who gave obedience to the elemental of Mount Moriah in return for perpetual ethnic identity for his progeny. We may affirm that this elemental kept its part of the bargain, since no "peoples" among Abraham's contemporaries still survive with identity intact, save for Abraham's own. But meanwhile the exclusivity of belief the pact demanded has infected the entire planet with the intolerance consequent to it. Aside from this, the identity Yahweh thus guaranteed has not always produced unmixed blessings, and in any event every human has an ancestry that goes back as far, even if we do not all know or care just how our 200-times-greatgrandparents carried out their worship.

It does credit, I suppose, to Mount Moriah's efficacy as a power spot that the struggle for its possession by the various branches of Abraham's progeny continues to this day, making it the most likely focal point for Crimson Apocalypse and the Death of Earth in Fire. This provides all the justification a sorcerer needs to treat any energy locus discrete enough to be articulate according to the standard procedure of naming, binding, and making the entity at least tractable to his or her will. If the sorcerer cannot do this, he or she should banish and withdraw to train and develop self until he or she can. If the sorcerer should succumb to any display by a power, even the most impressive, and give over some aspect of will in return for that power's favor, he or she runs a risk directly proportional to the magnitude of the power. We must bind all spirits that we intend to work with. If we cannot do so, then we must change our plans and leave them alone, lest they infect the whole planet with their unbalanced pretensions.

But then I won't suggest that a spirit, once bound, no longer needs safe handling. You should always act with civility when you deal with them, but must never show subservience or ingratiation. You must never allow their shapes, on whatever plane you perceive them, to superimpose themselves on your own form as it appears on that plane—to invade it, as it were. And you must only allow spirits to speak when spoken to, unless their special function is giving warning. Even in this special case, you'll do better to use them to charge a talisman that you can put on and take off than to give a personified paranoia such wide latitude. And you must never really *trust* the spirits, since they will always try to advance themselves, even at the price of throwing the total you into imbalance. As Abraham the Jew of Worms put it in *The Book of the Sacred Magic of Abramelin the Mage*:

> If they know that a man is inclined to Vanity and Pride, they will humiliate themselves before him, and push that humility unto excess, and even unto idolatry, and this man will glory herein and become intoxicated with conceit, and the matter will not end without him commanding them some pernicious thing of such a nature that ultimately thenceforth will be derived that sin which will make the man the Slave of the Demon. (pp. 254–255)

In all dealings with spirits—from their identification and initial binding to their day-to-day management and the interpretation of uncanny events that may involve them—your Holy Guardian Angel will provide you with essential assistance and support. The

Knowledge and Conversation of one's Angel is an essential initiation, and thus an immediate priority, for any who choose to work according to the spirit model.

# V. Using Power

Assuming then:

- that the wizard has honed his or her subtle body, will and personality dynamics so his or her psyche has become an efficient receptacle, tool and conduit to store, move, and manipulate power according to the wizard's will,
- that the wizard's nominal power exchanges with his or her fellow humans are equitable and unrestricted by sentimentality,
- that with exquisite sensitivity the wizard has gathered energy from the natural world and either stored it or applied it to attain optimum physical and spiritual well-being,
- and that he or she has avoided compromising the integrity of his or her psychic structure through careless or imprudent dealings with spirits,

then this wizard's conjurations will have acquired genuine effect, beneficent or malign, depending on his or her ability to apply them properly to his or her circumstances.

This is simply to say that once we have acquired magickal power in an ethical way, we have to take care to use it ethically, conjuring to manufacture a world that gives us joy to live in instead of trashing the one we have now in a futile attempt at making it behave in just the way we like.

The conjurations that carry the most ethical weight also tend to carry the greatest weight of human desire: those involving money, love and vengeance. We must never take lightly that which all humanity hates or desires. If you expect to use magick to make these light, then puff them about to your own advantage before they sink back down into consequence, then you expect to do evil.

Thus we must pause to face the question of black magick, my definition of which is as follows:

## Black magick is conjuring to get something for nothing.

And while such magick brings the desired result with inevitable fatality, the price can taint your whole life, and in the end the result probably won't give you what you really wanted after all.

Before all else, "something for nothing" violates the laws of physics, defying both the laws of thermodynamics and Newton's Third Law. And when one conjures for money, love or vengeance, these laws stand before us stark and essentially inescapable. Let us begin with money, where the concept of "something for nothing" has its origin.

We can use two approaches to apply magick to gain prosperity.

We can conjure to help inspire, produce or market something that people naturally want to buy. Here the magician clearly seeks to make wealth, rather than just get it, and so the magician produces no distortions in the ethical field. He or she uses magick in the most positive way possible.

Or we can just conjure for cash. The magician here creates a stress that tends to liquidate whatever value he or she has managed to accumulate, if only as a member of that vast insurance pool that is modern society. Thus a conjuration for cash generally results in either an insurance settlement, a legacy or a favorable legal judgment. But whatever the mechanism, the event that brings the money or justifies its payment will cause no trivial hurt, and so the magician will earn every penny. The magician may never want for anything again, except for the ability to move his feet.

Of course we can use more devious ways to address the problem, for instance those involving some financial institution that depends heavily on fate, chance or delusion—for instance the stock market or the dog track. The sorcerer works the magick to give his or her financial instrument an occult advantage over its competition. Of course if you work to promote your company or your dog—you being owner, trainer, chief financial officer or an engineer with stock options—your performance of this magick would have no moral taint, simply because you would have a rapport with the corporation/animal and so would possess the knowledge and sensitivity to apply power as part of a deliberate strategy. You would use your magick to make wealth—a profitable company, a fast dog—rather than just pluck cash from Fortune's Wheel. But to just sit at trackside and throw power at the poor beast in hopes of beating out your fellow humans in an essentially parimutuel division of spoils seems to verge on the black half of our art. So you send your dog some power. Will it win, or will it dislocate its hip from having more strength than it can handle? So you empower your chosen corporation. Will it inspire new heights of innovative product design, or an ill-advised advertising campaign? In the end, you won't gain so very much more profit than what you would have gotten without using magick, but your karmic involvement will be enormous.

Now I should stress that none of these considerations have anything to do with the use of magick to help you recognize a winner when you see one, since the acquisition of information seems to transcend the moral plane. But of course magick done for this can never be infallible. The question of timing can always vex us. The horse might be a winner, but as a five-year-old gelding, which doesn't help much with the Kentucky Derby. Thus information magick works best for someone already familiar with the financial institution in question—race track or bourse—rather than for one who just jumped in in ignorance in order to exploit the randomity. If your uncle first took you to the dog track on your sixth birthday, and you've been following the puppies ever since, then by all means invoke Diana to learn more about her hounds. But she's not such a friendly goddess that she welcomes pushy neophytes who have no sense of devotion to her beasts, but just want to make some bucks.

So much for money, then. What of magick done to obtain the love of our fellow humans?

Here the ethical implications depend on what you specifically expect to get.

Perhaps you will conjure for sexual release—purely physical, no future required. Then the magick will simply enable you to lower your standards, and the ethical consequences here need no occult interpretation. But if you desire intimacy with individuals who resist you, and use magick to get it, then the consequences turn treacherous. After all, if they attract you and yet you remain apart, then some source of alienation or aversion must oppose that intimacy. This could consist of anything from class differences to body odor, from an Oedipus complex to an inconvenient spouse, from poverty to an attraction to a sex opposite your own. The magick will in no way overcome these difficulties. Instead it will cause you to begin sexual relations in spite of them, and so will they taint all aspects of your life together. So if she doesn't like your job but you conjure her into your bed anyway, she'll spend more money than you can earn and when you make love she'll nag you to get something better even after you've both come. And then you'll get her pregnant, so you can expect to work about three jobs at a time for the next eighteen years.

The alternative, as with the money magick, is to use magick to manufacture a relationship that works. Conjure to meet someone compatible, perform divinations to search out likely pitfalls and find out how to bridge them, do deep astral research on your own psyche to uncover any demons working to thwart your domestic happiness. In short, realize that relationships require work, and then use magick to get it done more thoroughly and efficiently.

Our final high energy goal for conjuring is vengeance. When one sends a curse, one launches a packet of disruptive psychic energy against one's opponent, a demon that will corrode and unravel the victim's subtle body until he or she falls prey to accident, sickness or financial disaster. By using the occult arts to carry out this retribution, the wizard assumes that he or she will evade detection and civil penalty. Essentially the wizard attempts to rise above Newton's Third Law, as if one could strike with force without having to absorb an equal amount. But any attempt to evade this rule merely moves its action to another plane. When one kills with a knife, the handle pushes back with as much force as the tip pushes in, but the point is designed to penetrate, and the handle to blunt. So the reaction goes to the social plane of police and law, with the particular risk that the knife itself will point out the one who used it. With magick the act of vengeance is occult, which is to say, *hidden*—hidden from both the precaution of the target and the disapproval of authority. But this also makes the Newtonian reaction less obvious, and thus harder to duck.

To generalize, in any hostile conjuration the wizard becomes vulnerable to whatever he or she sends out, both from familiarity with it and from his or her link to it as its creator. The wizard emanates it, and so does he or she have an existential rapport with it. Though he or she might use ritual means to sever this rapport, the wizard's very knowledge of its existence provides an opening it may use to reestablish the connection. If the wizard sends a spirit brimming with destructive energy out against the hated opponent, and yet for some reason it cannot attach itself, the wizard will have to deal with its frustrated impetus.

On the other hand, if the wizard chooses instead to attack the target with a stream of his or her own energy—an extension of self rather than a discrete spiritual projectile—and thus confront Newton head-on, he or she risks having it bitten off and swallowed, then digested to reinforce the vigor of the enemy.

One can use many strategies to evade these difficulties, but most boil down to having better leverage and more power than the opponent.

Leverage provides a strong center and a firm footing for both launching blows and deflecting them. We can obtain excellent leverage simply by being in the right, for then we will have no vulnerability to doubt, which can cripple psychic coherence. Conversely, if an attacker has a no justification for his or her act, he or she confronts the defense of innocence against spite, where the power sent finds no way to enter the target, but a wide avenue for reentering the one who sent it to begin with. Another source of leverage is a defensive position, since familiar surroundings and solid social ties provide a strong circle against outside penetration.

Thus magickal attack will not work as well against any sort of phlegmatic opponent—firm on his base, secure in his support, deliberate in his movements—but does better when used to trip up the galumphing madman.

A wizard's power, on the other hand, simply consists of his or her ability to perceive, generate, move, store, resist and reify psychic energy. It will give the wizard the ability to fabricate a demon of heart-rotting nastiness and direct that demon against an opponent. Power provides the opponent with the ability to recognize the omens that herald the demon's arrival, or to perceive its true nature at first glance, and thus gives the opponent the ability to banish and "be elsewhere" while it circles his or her aura. Power provides the ability to not remember having sent the demon when, baffled by the target's non-appearance, it comes home looking for other meat to eat: the one who fabricated it in the first place.

And then it gets down to who can wait the longest.

All this is simply to say that none of this is free. Curses work, but they are no more certain in their outcome than a knife fight or a contested divorce. Thus the ethics of the curse are no different from those of any other blood feud. The error that people make consists of assuming that they can escape retaliation through resort to magick. The person who supposes that he or she can evade inescapable psychic dynamics may be seen as evil, but the error has as much to do with simple slowness of wit and an ignorance of what magick involves. Magick can provide no sort of easy way out. Instead it offers a short cut for people who make themselves psychically prepared, an opportunity to exploit efficiencies unavailable to those who limit themselves to mundane operations. But magick gives us no license to violate basic conservation laws. To suppose that it does and then conjure or curse on that supposition simply guarantees some sort of correction. You will benefit your purse, your health and your self-esteem if you find out how these laws apply to your special case before you begin to conjure, lest you run hard up against them in a way you cannot forget. A knack for divination is essential here, a clear light with which to recognize our hubris before we provide it with sufficient energy to destroy us.

## VI. A Common Thread

For all the categories of occult behavior that I have thus far labeled "unethical"—vampirism, pacts with spirits, trying to get something for nothing—the overall motif consists of abandonment of self out of lust for an immediate result. Those who try to get something for nothing are so enamored of the result that they have no care for where this wonderful thing might come from, or whose loss is their gain. In the case of pacts, one is so desperate to have a power that one surrenders one's will to the spirit that can supply it. And with vampirism the erasure of personal distinction to satisfy one's hunger for vital force is the defining characteristic. The vampire acts as a cancer cell in the spiritual body of mankind—undifferentiated, voracious, malignant. Lust of result—spiritual satiation—is what feeding for the vampire is all about, and in the end the matted remnants of personalities long since digested are the vampire's doom.

It may seem ironic, or perhaps contrived, how I repeatedly describe lapses of magickal ethics being punished in ways that are poetically correct. The vampire is destroyed by the accumulated corruption of his victims. The one who makes a pact becomes the slave of the power desired. The black magician is destroyed as a direct consequence of getting what he conjures for. But the poetry has no mysterious origin. Magickal laws are like laws of physics. Violations are not punished by the exactions of an omnipotent deity or the coercions of parents, peers or society. Rather, they are punished when the insulting operation blows up in the perpetrator's face. Since magickal results occur in terms of human events rather than objects, the shrapnel from these explosions consists not of nuts and bolts and shards of glass, but of sharp edges of consequence that stick out of the victims in a grotesquely literary manner. Hence the poetry.

But not every argument with the laws of physics brings on an explosion. There can instead be a slow, grinding stress that never fractures, only compresses, until everything turns to sand and sawdust, a process that can seem so natural, so inevitable, that the people it happens to can only recognize it in retrospect, when they confuse it with old age.

## VII. Power Caught in the Cave

According to the story of Attis and the nymph, Attis was the consort of Cybele, the Great Mother of the Gods. Exposed as an infant on the banks of the river Gallus, he was nursed by a wild goat. He grew up like a flower, became a shepherd, and Cybele fell in love with him. She set the starry cap on his head and gave him freedom to dance and play, so long as he stayed on her side of the river. But he would not limit himself, and crossed over.

On the other side he met a nymph. She excited his lust and led him into her cave, dark and moist, where they joined in intercourse. When Cybele heard of his disobedience, she caused Attis to go mad. He castrated himself, left his genitals in the cave with the nymph, and crossed over the Gallus to rejoin the Great Mother.

Cybele was a primordial mother goddess indigenous to Asia Minor. She was first associated with her lover, Attis, in the 7th century b.c.e., when their cult was established in Phrygia in the uplands of central Anatolia and also on Mount Ida, near Troy. It may be that Attis was originally considered mortal, and his self-castration fatal without resurrection. But during the Roman Empire his position was elevated to that of full-fledged dying and rising god in the tradition of Tammuz and Baal. The Neoplatonic theurgists took his story as a defining myth, his castration symbolizing for them the entrapment of generative force within matter.

For the Neoplatonists, matter was the ultimate in non-being. Its only quality was extension, its every other likely attribute—even ductility and mass—being the product of form projected down onto it from a higher ontological level. Thus one would expect that such a complex, sophisticated and potent quality as that of generation would be wholly alien to it. And yet generation appears inseparable from matter, life spawning with seeming spontaneity straight out of the slime. Plotinus, the founder of Neoplatonism, offered a general explanation when he remarked that what enters matter "ceases to belong to itself." But why does such a high thing as generative force enter matter in the first place? Mature theurgy discovered its answer in the myth of Attis, and we may also find it of use in our modern magick. Even if the Neoplatonic notion of matter is dated in the light of quantum physics, there are traps aplenty in the corporate cave that is our modern Babylon, and the Attis dynamic tends to apply to these as well. It is fundamental and finds embodiment on all planes.

The theurgic Attis was given definitive treatments in the Emperor Julian's "Hymn to the Mother of the Gods" and in Sallustus's "Concerning the Gods and the Universe," both written in Greek in the 4th century.

On the myth's most mundane level of interpretation, Attis is a typical seasonal deity who springs forth in a vernal flood and then is cut down by dark, drought or cold. From this it follows for Julian that Attis represents an aspect of Helios, the sun's rays as they penetrate down into matter, "assigned as a sort of vehicle for the safe descent of our souls into this world of generation." That Cybele put a starry cap onto Attis' head implies that his origins were in the Highest, consistent with Helios's position as leader of the intellectual gods.[14] And both Julian and Sallustus interpret the River Gallus as *Gallaxias Kyklos*, the Milky Way. This in theurgic cosmology was the frontier between the eternal and the transitory. As Julian put it, it was the interface where "that which is subject to change mingles with the passionless revolving sphere of the fifth substance." "That which is subject to change" is the material world of the four elements, while "the fifth substance" is æther, divinity at its most substantial. Thus below æther "this fair intellectual god

---

[14] Beneath the intelligible gods (the Platonic forms), but above the level of soul.

Attis, who resembles the sun's rays," was forbidden to go. (165C) But he crossed over anyway.

He finds the nymph and she leads him to her cave. Julian tells us that the nymph and cave are "the dampness of matter." (165D) Sallustus adds that nymphs preside over the processes of generation. "But since it was necessary that the process of coming into being should stop and what was worse should not sink to the worst," the forces of creation severed the power of generation and gave it to "the world of becoming" and then, thus purified, ascended again to the divine realms. (p. 182)

"Worse," for Sallustus is any involvement at all of spirit with matter; "worst" is the total involvement of divinity in the world of affairs. In the story of Attis the theurgists found a near-Gnostic allegory explaining how this our world of change could have so much of eternity to it, yet still be so manifestly separate from the Higher Realms. It was their explanation for how matter—something they saw as definitively empty—could pump itself so full of vital force.

Here we encounter the origin of a fundamental bias that taints magick to this day: the notion that it is somehow improper, dangerous or even evil to use magick to influence our world of affairs. In this view magick may only be applied to "spiritual attainment"—the promotion of our journey back toward the One, the Absolute, Pure Cosmic Being. For this Neoplatonic mind-set, any other use of magickal power puts us in the same class as Attis, wasting our power to animate the intrinsically desolate. But this presumption of matter as formless oblivion is the Neoplatonists' greatest error, since they denigrate matter falsely. Modern physics has shown that matter is not a blackness without form, but instead an exquisite entanglement of Pure Light fit into perfectly balanced forms calibrated before the Beginning to make stars and planets and carbon-based life inevitable. Manifestation is thus nothing to denigrate, but rather something to exalt. It is a work in progress permeating the n-dimensions of space, and all the tools of sorcery are at hand to encourage this exaltation.

And yet the model of Attis and the nymph is still useful. It rises up out of an unconscious depth and so has a primal validity that mere quantum physics cannot gainsay. It's just that Plotinus and his successors could not penetrate to the substrata of the problem. Matter does not trap us; states of being do. Though these may seem less substantial than the weight of stuff that holds us down, they are more alluring, more difficult to see as traps, and easier to fall into—until all power to escape them has been drained and our wills rendered impotent.

In general these snares present themselves as circumstances which, if only we give them sufficient support, will blossom and bear fruit as perfect situations that will sustain us in comfort until the end of our days. What happens instead is that we sustain the circumstance with our own energy until we become exhausted, at which point we are either expelled from it or the whole thing falls in on itself, and upon ourselves also.

Consider, for example, the mood of an individual faced with a New Thing all full of potential and promise for glory. One's elders are baffled; never before has such a Thing been seen upon the face of the earth. One seems to be moving with a flood of energy fit to build a perfect world; if one is still young, there may even be intimations of immortality. Whether the New Thing be as it arose in San Francisco during the Summer of Love, across Europe in 1968, or in America with the blossoming of the Internet, in one way or another it seems that if oneself and one's fellows can only make this New World real, they will be masters of it and by extension All Things. But such a world only lasts for as long as their enthusiasm animates it. When it is gone—or even just slightly distracted—the world turns and they are left with something somehow tarnished or tattered: just another chamber within the Inferno of the Normal.

Of course such New Worlds are the exception, and really only come along every 25 years or so. But it's easy to enter the Attis-mode without them. Any situation we fall into while in the full bloom of youth will do, be it a career at XYZ, Inc., tenure track at the university, or a life of service to the military. In all such cases

one gives up youth to sustain policy, and by the time one realizes
one's error the spark is gone and it's time to begin one's midlife
crisis.

Nymphs such situations are, waiting in caves, though their
human lovers will be unable to recognize them as such until their
testicles are caught in the rocks and Father Time holds the knife.

Perhaps the best way to address this problem would be to contrast the desire to attain a state of being with a willingness to stake
one's life on a state of momentum.

The desire to attain a state of being is the desire for safety, for
rest, for stasis in a world that will endure without surprises. Of
course such a condition cannot be found outside the grave—or
cave—and so calls to mind that primal magickal admonition:

*Fear is failure and the forerunner of failure. Be therefore without fear,
for in the heart of a coward, virtue abideth not.*

I would note that the English word "virtue" has two meanings.
It stands for both "moral rectitude" and "intrinsic power." And
without intrinsic power, no person can consistently behave with
moral rectitude. But to devote power to the animation of a state of
being—to the creation of a specific world in defiance of its inevitable opposition—is to use power to resist uncertainty rather than
exploit it. To resist uncertainty is to affirm one's fear of it. And
when the world thus manufactured begins to crumble, then fear
will redouble and moral rectitude will be cast aside in a desperate
attempt to restore that security.

The alternative is the attainment of a state of enduring momentum. This is a matter of *doing* instead of *being*, which calls to mind
the English Chaos magician Peter J. Carroll's notion of Anontol-
ogy. This doctrine holds that "being" is an illusory concept, that all
things consist of elements of action, of "doing." This is certainly
the case at the material level, where the smallest bits of stuff apparently consist only of action spinning upon its own self. Thus it's
probably safe to say that more complex states of being are equally
processes, unities of action that hold together so long as there is a
flow-through of energy to sustain them—transitory phases of orga-

nization in an ongoing elaboration of chaos, like a hurricane or Jupiter's red spot. Since all is process, if one lusts after "being" one commits one's generative force to an organization that exists only to dissipate itself. But if one can instead identify with one's momentum through chaos, one can iterate through whole sequences of apparent organization without breaking stride. It is the ability to move through life without breaking stride, I think, that is the most immediate of virtue's many rewards—whether "virtue" be ethic or power—and reason enough in itself for wizards to take notice of it.

First published partially in *Der Golem*, no. 5, Kahla, 2001, as "Vom tugendhaften Zauberer," translated by Tula von Irminsul. First complete publication in *Wege aus der Grotte der Nymphen*, Bohmeier Verlag, Lübeck, 2002. This is this essay's first publication in English.

# Bibliography

Carroll, Peter J., *Liber Null & Psychonaut*, Samuel Weiser, York Beach, 1987

*Psybermagick*, Chaos International, London, 1995

Castaneda, Carlos, *The Teachings of don Juan*, Ballantine, New York, 1969

Chia, Mantak, *Awaken Healing Energy through Tao*, Aurora, New York, 1983

Crowley, Aleister, *Book Four*, Sangreal, Dallas, 1972

*The Book of Lies*, Samuel Weiser, New York, 1970

*The Book of the Law*, Samuel Weiser, New York, 1976

*The Confessions of Aleister Crowley*, Arkana, London, 1989

*Liber Agape & De Arte Magica*, Kadath Press, East Morton, 1986

*Liber Aleph*, Level Press, San Francisco, 1974

*Magick in Theory and Practice,* Castle, New York, n.d.

"The Ouija Board—A Note," *The International,* New York, October 1917, p. 319

Cumont, Franz, *Oriental Religions in Roman Paganism,* Dover, New York, 1956

Flavius Claudius Julianus, "Hymn to the Mother of the Gods," *The Works of the Emperor Julian*, (trans. by Wilmer Cave Wright), William Heinemann, London, and Macmillan, New York, 1913

Grieve, Mrs. M., *A Modern Herbal*, Dover, New York, 1971

Hartmann, Franz, *Paracelsus*, Kegan Paul, London, 1887

King, Francis, *The Rites of Modern Occult Magic*, Macmillan, New York, 1971

*The Lesser Key of Solomon: Goetia*, De Laurence, Chicago, 1916

Mace, Stephen, *Stealing the Fire from Heaven*, Dagon Productions, Phoenix, 2003

Macrobius Ambrosius Theodosius, *The Saturnalia* (trans. by Percival Vaughan Davies), Columbia University Press, New York & London, 1969

Mathers, S.L. MacGregor, *The Book of the Sacred Magic of Abramelin the Mage*, de Laurence, Chicago, 1948

Plotinus, "The Six Enneads" (trans. by Stephen MacKenna and B.S. Page), *Great Books of the Western World, No. 17*, Encyclopaedia Britannica, Chicago, 1952

Regardie, Israel, *The Golden Dawn*, Llewellyn, St. Paul, 1971

Spare, Austin Osman, *The Anathema of Zos*, Black Moon, Cincinnati, 1985

*The Book of Pleasure*, 93 Publishing, Montreal, 1975

*The Focus of Life*, Askin, London, 1976

Sallustus, "Concerning the Gods and the Universe" (trans. by A.D. Nock), *Hellenistic Religions,* Liberal Arts Press, 1953

Frater U.D., "Models of Magic," *Chaos International* no. 9, London, 1990

Wilson, Colin, *The Occult*, Vintage, New York, 1973

# About the Author

Stephen Mace was introduced to the study of sorcery in 1970, when a Tarot reading predicted an imminent disaster in his life. Three days later the State Police raided his apartment, confiscated his stock and trade, bound him with handcuffs, and locked him in their tomb/womb for six weeks. In the 35 years since he has dedicated himself to the discovery of the fundamental dynamics of the art, the better to empower individuals to defy the oppression of the State Apparatus. To this end he has written several books, including *Stealing the Fire from Heaven, Shaping Formless Fire* and *Seizing Power.*

# MORE BOOKS ON MAGIC

## SHAPING FORMLESS FIRE
*Distilling the Quintessence of Magick*
### by Stephen Mace

Magick depends upon no abstract philosophies, and doing it requires neither devotion to any god or demon nor knowledge of the "True Keys of the Mysteries." Instead it is a technique for recognizing and manipulating psychic energy, both within the psyche and outside it, and for acquiring the mental skills we need to do this effectively. *Shaping Formless Fire* presents this with a simple elegance that contradicts the notion that magick must remain a hidden art.

ISBN 1-56184-238-9

## SEIZING POWER
*Reclaiming Our Liberty Through Magick*
### by Stephen Mace

Mace explores the magick of using power to deal with the two institutions that seem to do the most to cripple our access to it: the Corporation and the State. Of these, the former is surely more odious than the latter, and infinitely less vital. Most odious of all, of course, is the carnal union of the two, but such depravity may tend toward the decline of both parties, and *Seizing Power* examines the dynamics of this process as well.

ISBN 1-56184-239-7

# MORE BOOKS ON MAGIC

## CONDENSED CHAOS
*An Introduction to Chaos Magic*
**by Phil Hine**
*Foreword by Peter J. Carroll*

"... the most concise statement ... of the logic of modern magic. Magic, in the light of modern physics, quantum theory and probability theory is now approaching science. We hope that a result of this will be a synthesis so that science will become more magical and magic more scientific."
— William S. Burroughs, author of *Naked Lunch*

"... a tour de force."— Ian Read, Editor, *Chaos International*

ISBN 1-56184-117-X

## CEREMONIAL MAGIC & THE POWER OF EVOCATION
**by Joseph C. Lisiewski, Ph.D.**
*Introduced by C.S. Hyatt, Ph.D.*

*Ceremonial Magic* lays bare the simplest of Grimoires, the Heptameron of Peter de Abano. Its Magical Axioms, extensive Commentaries, copious notes, and personal instructions to the reader make this a resource that no serious student of Magic can afford to be without. It is all here, as in no other Grimoire. Use its instructions and the world of evocation and personal gratification are well within your grasp!

ISBN 1-56184-197-8

# New Falcon Publications

**Invites You to Visit Our Website:**
**http://www.newfalcon.com**

At the Falcon website you can:

- Browse the online catalog of all of our great titles
- Find out what's available and what's out of stock
- Get special discounts
- Order our titles through our secure online server
- Find products not available anywhere else including:
  - One of a kind and limited availability products
  - Special packages
  - Special pricing
- Get free gifts
- Join our email list for advance notice of New Releases and Special Offers
- Find out about book signings and author events
- Send email to our authors (including the elusive Dr. Christopher Hyatt!)
- Read excerpts of many of our titles
- Find links to our author's websites
- Discover links to other weird and wonderful sites
- And much, much more

**Get online today at http://www.newfalcon.com**